kids' birthday cakes

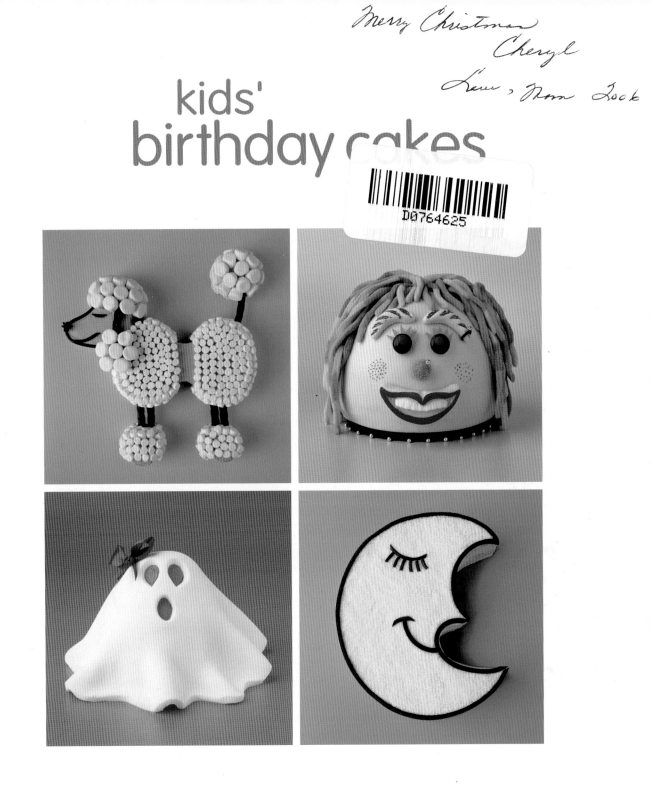

THE AUSTRALIAN
Women's Weekly

Ask me what's the favourite part of my job and my answer would have to be, "See this book!" I love baking, and I'm just crazy about every aspect of creating children's birthday cakes – from seeing what clever and colourful ideas the Test Kitchen team dreams up, to the practical challenge of getting the idea down on paper, to the final step when the wide eyes of the birthday child say it all. I'd particularly like to thank Kimberley Coverdale, Kelly Cruickshanks and Amira Georgy for their major contribution to this very special book.

Pamela Clark

Food Director

contents

the magic toadstool

cake

2 x 340g packets buttercake mix
35cm x 50cm prepared board (page 112)
1½ quantities butter cream (page 112)
yellow and pink colouring
15cm-round cardboard

decorations

4 pink Fruit Sticks
2 spearmint leaves
8 mini heart lollies
1 yellow Fruit Stick
25 large heart lollies
24 silver cachous
3 large white marshmallows
3 white marshmallows
1 teaspoon cocoa powder
assorted mini fairy statues

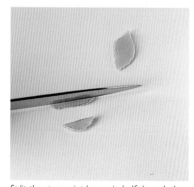

Position the large cake on the small cake, then spread pink butter cream over toadstool cap

Split the spearmint leaves in half through the centre then slice the halves into three pieces

1 Preheat oven to moderate; grease 1.25-litre (5 cup) and 2.25-litre (9 cup) pudding steamers. Make cake according to directions on packet, pour mixture into steamers until three-quarters full; bake smaller pudding in moderate oven about 35 minutes and larger pudding about 55 minutes. Stand cakes in steamers 5 minutes; turn onto wire rack to cool. Using serrated knife, level cake tops.

2 Place small cake on board. Tint ½ of the butter cream with yellow colouring; spread all over cake for toadstool stem.

3 Position large cake on cardboard round, cut-side down. Position large cake on toadstool stem for toadstool cap. Tint remaining butter cream with pink colouring; spread all over cap.

4 Place pink Fruit Sticks, side by side, on flat surface; trim tops of sticks to make rounded door. Position on toadstool stem for door.

5 Split spearmint leaves in half through centre; slice halves into three pieces, as shown. Use centre pieces for stems and side pieces as leaves; position around toadstool stem. Position two mini heart lollies at top of each spearmint stem for flowers.

6 Cut yellow Fruit Stick into thin strips; using a little water, position on two large heart lollies; position on toadstool stem for windows.

7 Position six large heart lollies on board at front of toadstool for path. Decorate toadstool cap with cachous and remaining large heart lollies.

8 Using a little butter cream, attach large marshmallows on top of smaller marshmallows, sprinkle with sifted cocoa powder; position around toadstool. Decorate toadstool with fairy statues as desired.

whirlipop

cake

340g packet buttercake mix
27cm x 60cm prepared board (page 112)
1 quantity butter cream (page 112)
yellow colouring

decorations

icing sugar mixture
500g ready-made soft icing
green and red colouring
3.5cm x 85cm orange ribbon
38cm dowelling

1 Preheat oven to moderate; grease and line (page 110) deep 17cm-round cake pan. Make cake according to directions on packet, pour into pan; bake in moderate oven about 45 minutes. Stand cake in pan 5 minutes; turn onto wire rack to cool. Using serrated knife, level cake top.

2 Place cake on board, cut-side down.

3 Tint butter cream with yellow colouring; spread all over cake.

4 On surface dusted with icing sugar, knead icing until smooth. Knead green colouring into ⅓ of the icing; roll into 1cm-thick cord. Enclose remaining icing in plastic wrap; reserve. Cut cord in half; cover both halves with plastic wrap. Repeat with reserved icing, tinting ½ of the icing red and ½ of the icing yellow.

5 Pinch one cord of each colour together, twist the cords by rotating them; cover with plastic wrap. Repeat with remaining three cords.

6 Starting from centre of cake, spiral one length of twisted cord, as shown. Join end of remaining twisted cord to first twisted cord by gently pinching and moulding cords together; continue spiralling twisted cord to cover cake.

7 Tie ribbon into a bow around dowelling; insert dowelling slightly into cake for lollipop stick.

tip You can paint the dowelling with non-toxic paint, if you like.

Place cake on the board, cut-side down, then spread the yellow butter cream over cake

Pinch the three cords together at one end, then twist cords together by rotating them

Starting from centre of cake, spiral twisted cord to cover the top of cake

echidna ice-cream cake

cake

3.5 litres choc-chip ice-cream, softened
1 cream-filled chocolate sponge finger, chilled

decorations

200ml milk chocolate Ice Magic
2 x 200g packets chocolate finger biscuits
100g dark chocolate, grated coarsely
2 green Smarties
21cm x 28cm prepared board (page 112)

1. Line 2.25-litre (9 cup) pudding steamer with plastic wrap; press softened ice-cream into steamer. Cover; freeze about 1 hour or until ice-cream re-sets.
2. Turn steamer upside down on baking-paper-lined tray. Remove steamer and plastic wrap from ice-cream.
3. Working quickly, trim 2cm from sponge finger; position at base of cake for nose. Using Ice Magic, coat nose and face in chocolate, as shown; stand until chocolate is almost set. Using sharp knife, trim away any excess chocolate. (Return to freezer if necessary).
4. Working quickly, push finger biscuits into ice-cream body; sprinkle between biscuits with grated chocolate.
5. Using a little Ice Magic, secure Smarties to echidna for eyes.
6. Freeze echidna until ready to serve. Using egg slides, transfer echidna from baking paper to board.

tips Use a good quality ice-cream; actual varieties of ice-cream differ from manufacturer to manufacturer depending on the quantities of air and fat that have been incorporated into the mixture.
Once the ice-cream softens and melts slightly, it takes up less space – that is why 3.5 litres of ice-cream can fit into a 2.25-litre pudding steamer.

Place steamer, upside down, on baking-paper-lined tray; remove steamer and plastic wrap

Using Ice Magic, coat the nose and face, then stand until the chocolate almost sets

Trim any excess chocolate from the echidna's nose and face with a sharp-pointed knife

Working quickly, push the chocolate finger biscuits into the ice-cream for echidna's spikes

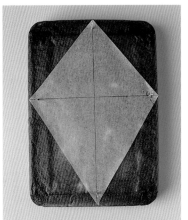

Place the cake cut-side down then, using the paper pattern, cut the kite from cake

go fly a kite

cake

3 x 340g packets buttercake mix
34cm x 43cm prepared board (page 112)
2½ quantities butter cream (page 112)
yellow, red, green and orange colouring

decorations

1 black licorice strap
50cm red ribbon
50cm purple ribbon
50cm orange ribbon
50cm green ribbon
1m rope
icing sugar mixture
250g ready-made soft icing

Using toothpicks as a guide, spread coloured butter creams over the kite quadrants

1 Preheat oven to moderate; grease and line (page 110) deep 26cm x 36cm baking dish. Make cake according to directions on packet, pour into dish; bake in moderate oven about 1 hour. Stand cake in dish 10 minutes; turn onto wire rack to cool. Using serrated knife, level cake top.

2 Using paper pattern (page 112) from pattern sheet, cut kite from cake, cut-side down. Position cake on board, cut-side down; discard remaining cake.

3 Place two lines of toothpicks in cake, connecting opposing corners of kite, as shown. Tint ¼ of the butter cream with yellow colouring, ¼ with red colouring, ¼ with green colouring and ¼ with orange colouring.

4 Using toothpicks as a guide, spread tinted butter creams over top and side of each kite quadrant; remove and discard toothpicks.

5 Cut licorice into thin strips; position around each coloured quadrant and edge of kite.

6 Using coloured ribbons, tie bows onto rope; position on board.

7 On surface dusted with icing sugar, knead icing until smooth; roll icing until 3mm thick. Using 4cm and 5cm flower cutters, cut clouds from icing. Position clouds on board around kite.

Roll the icing until 3mm thick then, using flower cutters, cut clouds from the icing

11

for you!

cake

340g packet buttercake mix
1 quantity butter cream (page 112)
yellow and pink colouring
40cm x 50cm prepared board (page 112)

decorations

2 x 250g packets coloured marshmallows
5 giant purple Smarties
7 giant pink Smarties
icing sugar mixture
350g ready-made soft icing
green colouring
pink bow
16 spearmint leaves

1 Preheat oven to moderate; line 12-hole (⅓ cup/80ml) muffin pan with
   paper patty cases. Make cake according to directions on packet, pour
   ¼ cup mixture into each hole; bake in moderate oven about 20 minutes.
   Stand cakes in pan 5 minutes; turn onto wire rack to cool.

2 Tint ½ of the butter cream with yellow colouring; spread over five cakes.
   Tint remaining butter cream with pink colouring; spread over remaining cakes.

3 Using scissors, cut 24 yellow marshmallows and 18 pink marshmallows in
   half. Squeeze ends of each marshmallow together to form petals, as shown.
   Decorate yellow cakes with six or seven pink marshmallow petals and
   pink cakes with six or seven yellow marshmallow petals.

4 Position purple Smarties in pink flower centres; position pink Smarties
   in yellow flower centres. Position flowers on board.

5 On surface dusted with icing sugar; knead icing until smooth. Knead
   green colouring into icing; divide icing into quarters. Roll ¼ of the icing
   into 5mm thick cord. Enclose remaining icing in plastic wrap; reserve.
   Cut icing cord into three uneven lengths; position on board. Repeat
   with reserved icing to make 12 stems in total.

6 Pinch stems together near ends; secure bow with a little butter cream.
   Position spearmint leaves along stems; secure with a little butter cream.

*Using scissors, cut the marshmallows in half
then squeeze the ends together to form petals*

hey diddle diddle

cake

2 x 340g packets buttercake mix
33cm-round prepared board (page 112)
1 quantity butter cream (page 112)
yellow colouring

decorations

1 black licorice strap
½ cup (110g) white sugar
yellow colouring

1 Preheat oven to moderate; grease and line (page 110) deep 22cm-round cake pan. Make cake according to directions on packet, pour into pan; bake in moderate oven about 50 minutes. Stand cake in pan 5 minutes; turn onto wire rack to cool. Using serrated knife, level cake top.
2 Using paper pattern (page 112) from pattern sheet, cut moon from cake, cut-side down. Place cake on board, cut-side down; discard remaining cake.
3 Tint butter cream with yellow colouring; spread all over cake.
4 Cut licorice into thin strips; position on cake for moon outline, eye and mouth.
5 Place sugar and yellow colouring in small plastic bag; rub colouring into sugar until evenly coloured, sprinkle evenly over moon face.

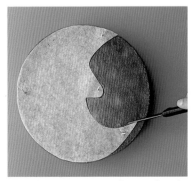
Using the paper pattern, cut the moon from the cake, cut-side down, with a small serrated knife

Tint the butter cream with yellow colouring then spread the butter cream all over the cake

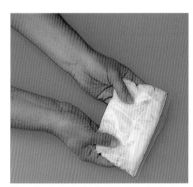
Place the sugar and colouring in a plastic bag, then rub together until sugar is evenly coloured

15

Using a serrated knife, trim the bottom of the steamer cake to make more rounded

Using a large palette knife, spread the red butter cream all over the ladybird's body

Position the muffin against the ladybird's body, for head, then spread with black butter cream

lazy ladybird

cake

340g packet buttercake mix
25cm x 30cm prepared board (page 112)
1 quantity butter cream (page 112)
black and red colouring

decorations

1 black licorice strap
14 chocolate freckles
2 x 15cm (3mm) black chenille sticks (pipe cleaners)
2 yellow Smarties

1 Preheat oven to moderate; grease one hole of 12-hole (1/3 cup/80ml) muffin pan and 1.25-litre (5 cup) pudding steamer. Make cake according to directions on packet, pour 1/4 cup of mixture into muffin hole and remaining mixture into pudding steamer; bake muffin in moderate oven about 20 minutes and steamer cake about 35 minutes. Stand cakes in pans 5 minutes; turn onto wire rack to cool. Using serrated knife, level steamer cake top.

2 Using serrated knife, cut segment from muffin, as shown; trim bottom of steamer cake to make more rounded, as shown. Place cake on board, top-side down.

3 Tint 1/4 cup of butter cream with black colouring and remaining butter cream with red colouring. Spread red butter cream all over body of ladybird.

4 Position muffin against body for head, secure with a little butter cream; spread all over with black butter cream. Pull an outside strip of licorice from the strap; position along centre of body. Position freckles on body.

5 Curl one end of each chenille stick; position on cake for antennae. Position Smarties on cake for eyes.

ginger neville

cake

2 x 340g packets buttercake mix
40cm-round prepared board (page 112)
2 quantities butter cream (page 112)
orange colouring

decorations

2 large white marshmallows
1 black licorice strap
1 giant blue Smartie, halved
8 x 15cm (3mm) black chenille sticks (pipe cleaners)
1 green bow

1. Preheat oven to moderate; grease and line (page 110) deep 22cm-round cake pan and 8cm x 25cm bar cake pan. Make cake according to directions on packet, divide mixture between pans so both mixtures are to the same depth; bake round cake in moderate oven about 50 minutes and bar cake about 25 minutes. Stand cakes in pans 5 minutes; turn onto wire rack to cool.
2. Using paper pattern (page 112) from pattern sheet, cut ears and face from cakes, top-side up, as shown.
3. Assemble cake pieces on board, top-side up, to form cat; discard remaining cake.
4. Using toothpicks, mark out centre stripe between ears. Using small serrated knife on the diagonal, trim about 1cm around edge of face.
5. Tint ½ of the butter cream with orange colouring to make light orange. Tint ½ of the remaining butter cream with orange colouring to make dark orange; leave remainder of butter cream plain.
6. Spread light orange butter cream all over cake. Spread all but 1 tablespoon of the dark orange butter cream over ears and stripe.
7. Spread 1 tablespoon of the plain butter cream for tips of ears and inside stripe. Swirl remaining tablespoon of the dark orange butter cream and all of the remaining plain butter cream together for marbled effect; dab over cat's cheeks to create fur.
8. Trim marshmallows into eye shapes; position on cake. Cut small piece of the licorice into thin strips for outline of eye. Cut two small pieces of the licorice for eyelashes. Position Smartie halves for eye irises.
9. Cut small piece of the licorice for nose and mouth. Position chenille sticks on cake for whiskers. Place bow under cat's chin.

Place the paper patterns on the cakes, then secure them with toothpicks to hold in place

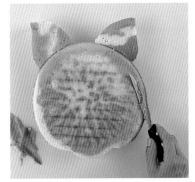

Using a small serrated knife on the diagonal, trim about 1cm off the edge of cat's face

Spread all but 1 tablespoon of the dark orange butter cream over ears and stripe

19

critters & crawlers

cake

340g packet buttercake mix
1½ quantities butter cream
**   (page 112)**
orange, blue, pink, green, violet
**   and yellow colouring**

decorations

BEE

3 black jelly beans
2 banana Runts
1 black licorice strap
white glossy decorating gel

BUTTERFLY

2 yellow jelly beans
4 chocolate freckles
2 banana Runts
black glossy decorating gel

TURTLE

1 green Sour Ball
2 green Runts
1 green Oompa
2 spearmint leaves
black glossy decorating gel
red glossy decorating gel

SPIDER

1 giant Jaffa
1 Jaffa
1 black licorice strap
black glossy decorating gel

DRAGONFLY

3 raspberries
4 strawberries & creams
2 Jelly Tots
2 orange Crazy Bananas
black glossy decorating gel

CATERPILLAR

6 orange Runts
2 spearmint leaves
black glossy decorating gel

1 Preheat oven to moderate; line six holes of 12-hole (⅓ cup/80ml) muffin pan with paper patty cases. Make cake according to directions on packet, pour ¼ cup of mixture into each hole; bake in moderate oven about 20 minutes. Stand patty cakes in pan 5 minutes; turn onto wire rack to cool.

2 Divide butter cream among six small bowls. Tint each bowl of butter cream with one of the suggested colours: orange, blue, pink, green, violet and yellow.

3 BEE Spread orange butter cream over one patty cake. Position black jelly beans and banana Runts alternately for body. Cut wings from licorice strap. Using white glossy decorating gel, pipe parallel lines on wings; position on either side of body. Cut 1cm piece from licorice strap, cut into thin pieces; position for pincers. Using white glossy decorating gel, dot eyes on bee.

4 BUTTERFLY Spread blue butter cream over one patty cake. Position yellow jelly beans for body; position freckles for wings. Position banana Runts for antennae. Using black glossy decorating gel, dot eyes on butterfly.

5 TURTLE Spread pink butter cream over one patty cake. Position Sour Ball for shell; position Runts for tail. Position Oompa for head; position spearmint leaves for flippers. Using black glossy decorating gel, dot spots on shell; using red glossy decorating gel, dot eyes on turtle.

6 SPIDER Spread green butter cream over one patty cake. Position giant Jaffa for body; position Jaffa for head. Cut licorice into thin strips, cut eight 3cm pieces from licorice strips; position for legs. Using black glossy decorating gel, dot eyes on head and draw line on back of spider.

7 DRAGONFLY Spread violet butter cream over one patty cake. Position raspberries for body; position strawberries & creams for wings. Trim Jelly Tots for eyes; position on front raspberry. Position Crazy Bananas for antennae. Using black glossy decorating gel, dot pupils on Jelly Tots.

8 CATERPILLAR Spread yellow butter cream over one patty cake. Position orange Runts on cake for body. Split spearmint leaves in half through centre; position for leaves. Using black glossy decorating gel, dot eyes and mouth on caterpillar.

tip The cake mix is enough to make 12 patty cakes, so decorate the other six patty cakes with your own favourite critters & crawlers.

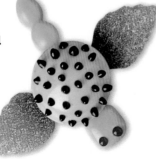

wicked wizard's hat

cake
3 x 340g packets buttercake mix
43cm x 47cm prepared board (page 112)
2 quantities butter cream (page 112)
blue colouring

decorations
silver cardboard
1 black licorice strap
100g white chocolate Melts, melted
yellow colouring
coloured sprinkles

1 Preheat oven to moderate; grease and line (page 110) deep 26cm x 36cm baking dish. Make cake according to directions on packet, pour into dish; bake in moderate oven about 1 hour. Stand cake in dish 10 minutes; turn onto wire rack to cool. Using serrated knife, level cake top.

2 Using paper pattern (page 112) from pattern sheet, cut hat from cake, cut-side down.

3 Assemble cake on board, cut-side down, to form hat; discard remaining cake.

4 Tint butter cream with blue colouring; spread all over cake.

5 Trace buckle shape at right; transpose onto silver cardboard, then cut out shape. Weave licorice strap through buckle; position on cake.

6 Trace the stars, above right, onto baking paper. Combine melted chocolate and yellow colouring in small bowl. Spoon into piping bag (page 115); pipe onto tracings of stars. Top ½ of the stars with coloured sprinkles; stand until stars set. Carefully lift stars from baking paper; position on cake.

tip You can also use star-patterned wrapping paper with a sheet of baking paper over it to use as a guide to making the stars.

Using the paper pattern, cut wizard's hat from cake, cut-side down, with a small serrated knife

Tint the butter cream with blue colouring; using a small palette knife, spread all over cake

Spoon chocolate into a piping bag; pipe onto tracings, sprinkle half with coloured sprinkles

Using the paper pattern, cut the pig's ears from one round cake, cut-side down

Assemble the cake pieces on board, cut-side down, to form the pig; discard remaining cake

Tint remaining pink butter cream with more pink colouring; spread over ears and cheeks

this little piggy

cake

2 x 340g packets buttercake mix
30cm-round prepared board (page 112)
1½ quantities butter cream (page 112)
pink colouring

decorations

2 large pink marshmallows
4 red fruit rings
2 giant black Smarties
2 aniseed rings
2 pink Smarties
2 musk sticks
1 artificial purple flower

1 Preheat oven to moderate. Grease one hole of Texas (¾ cup/180ml) muffin pan; grease and line (page 110) two deep 20cm-round cake pans. Make cake according to directions on packet, pour ½ cup of mixture into muffin hole then divide remaining cake mixture between round pans; bake muffin in moderate oven about 25 minutes and round cakes about 40 minutes. Stand cakes in pans 5 minutes; turn onto wire racks to cool. Using serrated knife, level cake tops.
2 Using paper pattern (page 112) from pattern sheet, cut pig's ears from one round cake, cut-side down.
3 Assemble cakes on board, cut-side down, to form pig; discard remaining cake.
4 Tint butter cream with pink colouring; spread ¾ of the butter cream all over cake. Tint remaining butter cream with more pink colouring to make a darker pink; spread over ears and cheeks.
5 Trim tip from each marshmallow, centre one fruit ring on each, press one black Smartie in centre for eyes; position on cake. Position aniseed rings, pink Smarties and half a fruit ring on cake to make nose. Use remaining fruit ring for mouth.
6 Thinly slice musk sticks lengthways; position on cake for eyelashes and tuft of hair. Position flower on cake.

tips Use a small amount of butter cream to attach the ears and nose to face. Make sure you buy the large marshmallows that look as if they've been piped, with a soft tip at the top.

whale of a day

cake

3 x 340g packets buttercake mix
31cm x 44cm prepared board (page 112)
2 quantities butter cream (page 112)
blue colouring

decorations

1 black licorice strap
1 giant black Smartie
7 x 15cm (3mm) white chenille sticks (pipe cleaners)

1 Preheat oven to moderate; grease and line (page 110) deep 26cm x 36cm baking dish. Make cake according to directions on packet, pour into pan; bake in moderate oven about 1 hour. Stand cake in dish 10 minutes; turn onto wire rack to cool. Using serrated knife, level cake top.

2 Using paper pattern (page 112) from pattern sheet, cut whale and ocean waves from cake, cut-side down. Place on board, cut-side down; discard remaining cake.

3 Tint ½ of the butter cream with blue colouring to make deep blue; spread all over whale body.

4 Tint ½ of the remaining butter cream with blue colouring to make mid-blue. Combine ½ of the remaining plain butter cream with 2 tablespoons of the mid-blue butter cream in small bowl to make light-blue butter cream. Spread mid-blue butter cream all over remaining cake.

5 Spread light-blue butter cream on mid-blue butter cream for waves. Spread remaining plain butter cream on peaks of waves.

6 Cut licorice into thin strips, position on cake for mouth; position Smartie on cake for eye. Position chenille sticks at blowhole for spout.

Using the paper pattern, cut the whale and ocean waves from the cake, cut-side down

Spread the mid-blue butter cream all over the remaining cake for the ocean waves

Using a palette knife, spread the remaining plain butter cream on the peaks of the waves

27

jungle fever

You need approximately 4 x 50g packets of Runts.

cake

3 x 340g packets buttercake mix
2 quantities butter cream (page 112)
green colouring
30cm-round prepared board (page 112)

decorations

icing sugar mixture
1kg ready-made soft icing
9 Flakes
17 banana Runts
10 pineapples
8 gummy feet
8 Cool Mints
red glossy decorating gel (page 115)
assorted toy animals

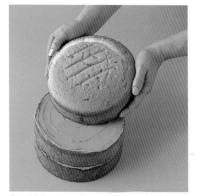

Spread the second trimmed cake with butter cream, then top with the untrimmed cake

Cut the leaves from icing then drape them over wooden spoons to curl and dry

Position the Flakes around the cake, then stack leaves on the cake so they overlap slightly

1 Preheat oven to moderate; grease and line (page 110) three deep 20cm-round cake pans. Make cake according to directions on packet, divide mixture among pans; bake in moderate oven about 40 minutes. Stand cakes in pans 5 minutes; turn onto wire racks to cool. Using serrated knife, level two cakes' tops so cakes are the same height.

2 Tint butter cream with green colouring; reserve ¾ of the butter cream.

3 Place one trimmed cake on board, cut-side down; spread with ½ of the remaining butter cream, top with remaining trimmed cake, cut-side down. Spread with remaining butter cream; top with remaining cake, top-side up. Spread reserved butter cream all over cakes.

4 Using paper pattern (page 112) from pattern sheet, transpose leaf onto cardboard and cut out. On surface dusted with icing sugar, knead icing until smooth. Knead green colouring into ½ of the icing to make light green; enclose remaining icing in plastic wrap, reserve. Roll icing until 3mm thick. Using cardboard leaf template and sharp-pointed knife, cut leaves from icing; drape over wooden spoons to slightly curl as they dry.

5 On surface dusted with icing sugar, knead green colouring into reserved icing to make dark green; roll until 3mm thick. Using same leaf template, cut leaves from icing; drape over wooden spoons to slightly curl as they dry.

6 Position Flakes around side of cake; stack slightly overlapping leaves on top of cake, securing each leaf with a little butter cream. Position banana Runts and pineapples around side of cake; position gummy feet around base of cake. Position Cool Mints, in pairs, for eyes around side of cake. Using decorating gel, dot pupils on Cool Mints.

7 Scatter assorted animals on and around cake.

tip It's best to make the leaves a few days ahead so that they thoroughly dry.

picture perfect

cake

2 x 340g packets buttercake mix
35cm-square prepared board (page 112)
2 quantities butter cream (page 112)

decorations

11cm-square photograph, laminated
1kg mixed lollies

1 Preheat oven to moderate; grease and line (page 110) deep 23cm-square cake pan. Make cake according to directions on packet, pour into pan; bake in moderate oven about 1 hour. Stand cake in pan 5 minutes; turn onto wire rack to cool. Using serrated knife, level cake top.
2 Place cake on board, cut-side down.
3 Spread butter cream all over cake.
4 Centre photograph carefully on top of cake.
5 Scatter mixed lollies all over cake; press lollies gently into butter cream.

tips You can use any photographic print you like, but remember to laminate it if you want it to remain after the cake is gone.
Use a selection of your favourite lollies to decorate this cake.

Spread the butter cream all over the cake then carefully centre the photograph on the cake

Using the paper patterns, cut the blade from cake and the handle from jam roll

Using a small serrated knife, cut blade on each side at an angle to make bevelled edges

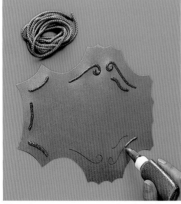

Using the paper pattern, cut the shield from cardboard then decorate with glitter glue

the pirate's dagger

cake

2 x 340g packets buttercake mix
400g jam roll
34cm x 43cm prepared board (page 112)
2½ quantities butter cream (page 112)
red and black colouring

decorations

23cm x 25cm piece gold cardboard
gold glitter glue
1.5m gold cord
craft glue
52 silver cachous
6 blue cachous
1 silver-covered sugared almond
3 gold cachous
3 pink Bo-Peep lollies
3 gold-covered sugared almonds
1 gold tassel

1 Preheat oven to moderate; grease and line (page 110) deep 23cm-square cake pan. Make cake according to directions on packet, pour into pan; bake in moderate oven about 1 hour. Stand cake in pan 5 minutes; turn onto wire rack to cool. Using serrated knife, level cake top.

2 Cut cake in half; place cakes together at the shorter edges, cut-side down, as shown. Using paper patterns (page 112) from pattern sheet, cut blade from cake and handle from jam roll.

3 Assemble cake pieces on board, cut-side down, to form dagger; discard remaining cake. Using small serrated knife, cut blade edges at an angle to make bevel, as shown.

4 Using paper pattern (page 112) from pattern sheet, cut shield from cardboard. Using gold glitter glue, draw pattern on shield. Cut 80cm from cord; using craft glue, attach cord around edge of shield. Position shield under handle of dagger.

5 Tint ⅖ of the butter cream with red colouring; spread all over handle of dagger. Tint remaining butter cream with black colouring to make grey; spread all over blade.

6 Decorate blade with silver and blue cachous and silver almond; decorate handle with gold cachous, Bo-Peeps and gold almonds.

7 Cut 20cm from remaining cord; wrap around join of blade and handle.

8 Tie remaining cord to tassel; loop around dagger.

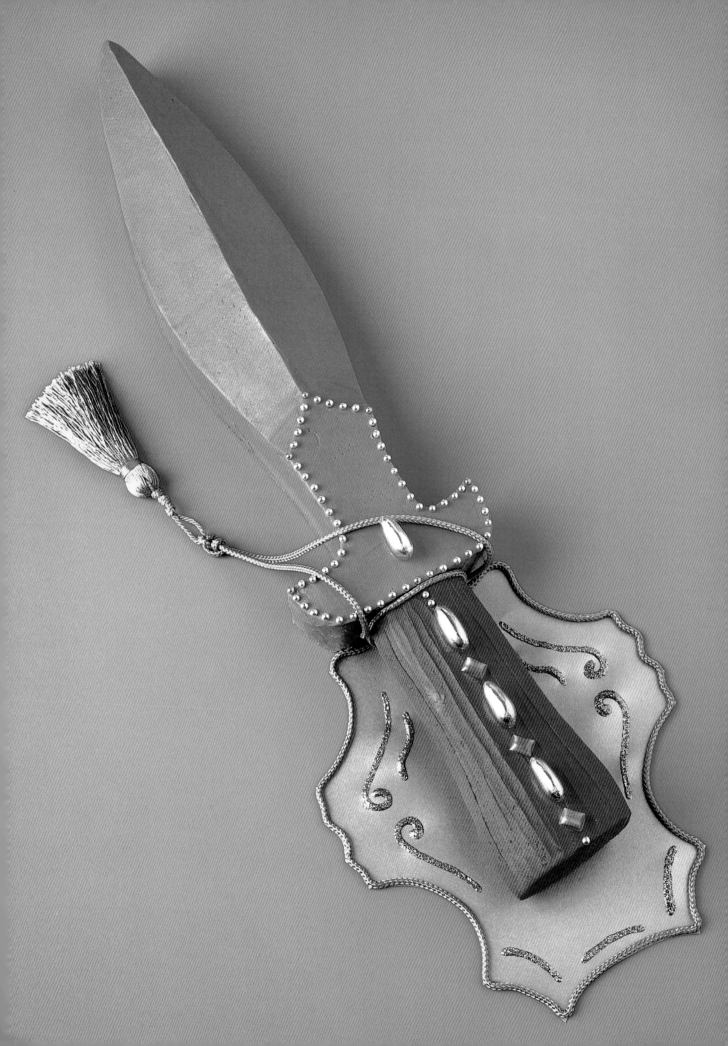

the penguin prince

cake

3 x 340g packets buttercake mix
35cm x 40cm prepared board (page 112)
2 quantities butter cream (page 112)
black, yellow and white colouring

decorations

2 giant black Smarties
1 black licorice strap
1 red bow tie

1 Preheat oven to moderate; grease and line (page 110) deep 26cm x 36cm
  baking dish. Make cake according to directions on packet, pour into dish;
  bake in moderate oven about 1 hour. Stand cake in dish 10 minutes; turn
  onto wire rack to cool. Using serrated knife, level cake top.

2 Using paper pattern (page 112) from pattern sheet, cut penguin
  from cake, cut-side down. Place penguin on board, cut-side down;
  discard remaining cake.

3 Using toothpick, mark penguin outlines onto cake.

4 Tint ½ of the butter cream with black colouring, ½ of the remaining
  butter cream with yellow colouring and remaining butter cream with
  white colouring.

5 Spread stomach and eyes with white butter cream, feet and beak with yellow
  butter cream and remaining top and sides of cake with black butter cream.

6 Position Smarties on cake for pupils. Trim licorice into a thin strip;
  position on beak. Position bow tie at penguin's neck.

Using the paper pattern, cut penguin from cake, cut-side down, with a small serrated knife

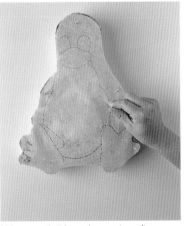
Using a toothpick, mark penguin outlines through the paper pattern onto the cake

Using the markings as a guide, spread the coloured butter creams onto the cake

Using the markings as a guide and a small serrated knife, cut a deep hollow into the cake

Spread the chocolate butter cream over the top and side of the cake, then fill the hollow

Swirl the chocolate around the inside of the steamer until it is evenly coated

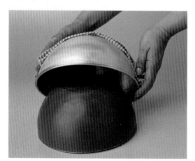

Use a hot cloth to briefly rub the outside of bowl, until the shell slips out of the steamer

party piñata
cake

340g packet buttercake mix
30cm-round prepared board (page 112)
1 quantity chocolate butter cream (page 112)

decorations

23 large chocolate coins
19 medium chocolate coins
13 small chocolate coins
150g rainbow choc-chips
½ teaspoon vegetable oil
450g milk chocolate Melts, melted
50g milk chocolate, melted
35g packet mini M&M's
50g packet Smarties
200g packet giant Smarties
toy hammer

1   Preheat oven to moderate; grease and line (page 110) deep 15cm-round cake pan. Make cake according to directions on packet, pour into pan until three-quarters full; bake in moderate oven about 45 minutes. Stand cake in pan 5 minutes; turn onto wire rack to cool. Using serrated knife, level cake top.

2   Position cake on board, cut-side down. Using ruler and toothpicks, mark 11cm circle in centre of cake. Using markings as a guide and small serrated knife, cut deep hollow into cake.

3   Spread chocolate butter cream all over cake; fill hollow with coins and ½ of the rainbow choc-chips.

4   To make chocolate shell: grease 2.25-litre (9 cup) pudding steamer with oil; place bowl in freezer 10 minutes. Place melted chocolate Melts in steamer; swirl chocolate to coat inside of steamer evenly. Continue swirling until chocolate begins to set and stops flowing around the steamer; try to keep the chocolate a uniform thickness, particularly at the edge. Stand until chocolate is almost set. Freeze until chocolate sets completely.

5   Carefully place pudding steamer with set chocolate shell over cake; using hot cloth, briefly rub outside of bowl. Chocolate shell will slip from bowl to completely cover cake.

6   Using melted milk chocolate, secure remaining rainbow choc-chips, mini M&M's, Smarties and giant Smarties to chocolate shell.

7   Allow birthday child to break chocolate shell open with toy hammer.

tip   Make patty cakes from any leftover cake mixture.

a yellow trampoline

cake

2 x 340g packets buttercake mix
33cm-round prepared board (page 112)
1 quantity butter cream (page 112)
green colouring

decorations

3 x 250g packets Fruit Sticks
icing sugar mixture
500g ready-made soft icing
yellow colouring
18cm cardboard circle
4 x 60g packets Chunky Raspberry Twister
assorted toy dolls

1 Preheat oven to moderate; grease and line (page 110) deep 22cm-round cake pan. Make cake according to directions on packet, pour into pan; bake in moderate oven about 50 minutes. Stand cake in pan 5 minutes; turn onto wire rack to cool. Using serrated knife, level cake top.

2 Position cake on board, cut-side down. Using ruler and toothpicks, mark a 17cm circle in centre of cake. Using markings as a guide, cut shallow hollow into cake with small serrated knife.

3 Tint butter cream with green colouring; spread all over cake.

4 Trim Fruit Sticks to the same height as cake; position around side of cake.

5 On surface dusted with icing sugar, knead icing until smooth. Knead yellow colouring into icing; roll until 5mm thick. Using the cardboard circle as a guide, cut circle from icing with sharp-pointed knife; position on centre of cake to cover hollow. Enclose remaining icing in plastic wrap.

6 Cut Raspberry Twisters in half lengthways; cut halves into 2.5cm pieces. Trim edges of pieces on an angle; position on cake for springs.

7 On surface dusted with icing sugar, roll reserved icing into 5mm cord; position around outside top edge of cake. Position dolls as desired.

Using the markings as a guide, cut a shallow hollow into the cake with a small serrated knife

Tint the butter cream with green colouring; using a palette knife, spread all over the cake

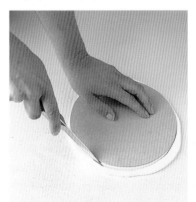

Using the cardboard circle as a guide, cut a circle from the icing with a sharp-pointed knife

Cut Raspberry Twisters in half lengthways then into 2.5cm pieces, trim the edges on an angle

39

express train

cake

2 x 340g packets buttercake mix
400g jam roll
22cm x 37cm prepared board (page 112)
2 quantities butter cream (page 112)
green colouring

decorations

2 red licorice straps
8 Carnival Pops
1 red Super Rope licorice
2 giant green Smarties
1 large yellow Sour Ball
22 yellow Smarties
8 red Smarties
1 Screw Pop
artificial spider's web

Cut a 2.5cm piece from one half of the square cake and trim a 3.5cm piece from the jam roll

Assemble the cakes on the board to form the train; discard any remaining cake and jam roll

1 Preheat oven to moderate; grease and line (page 110) deep 23cm-square cake pan. Make cake according to directions on packet, pour into pan; bake in moderate oven about 1 hour. Stand cake in pan 5 minutes; turn onto wire rack to cool. Using serrated knife, level cake top.

2 Cut square cake in half; cut 2.5cm piece from one half of square cake.

3 Cut 3.5cm piece from jam roll. Assemble cakes on board to form train, as shown; discard remaining cake.

4 Tint butter cream with green colouring; spread all over train.

5 Cut licorice strap into thin strips; using licorice, outline train's edges and make window on train.

6 Trim and discard sticks from Carnival Pops; position as wheels. Cut eight 1.5cm pieces from Super Rope; position between wheels as axle.

7 Cut two 8cm pieces from Super Rope; position at front of train for bumper. Position giant Smarties and Sour Ball at front of train for lights. Decorate train with yellow and red Smarties.

8 Place Screw Pop in position for funnel; place a little of the butter cream on top of funnel. Press the end of a piece of spider's web into the butter cream for smoke.

tip When it comes to eating this cake, remember that a small segment of stick is still embedded in each Carnival Pop (used for wheels).

huff & puff

cake

2 x 340g packets buttercake mix
31cm x 45cm prepared board (page 112)
1½ quantities butter cream (page 112)
pink colouring

decorations

1 red licorice strap
1 pink marshmallow
2 giant red Smarties
2 red Smarties
2 giant green Smarties
4 giant purple Smarties
5 purple Smarties
6 green Smarties
3 pink ice-cream wafers
Twinkle Sprinkles

1 Preheat oven to moderate; grease and line (page 110) deep 22cm-round cake pan, and grease two holes of 12-hole (¹/₃ cup/80ml) muffin pan. Make cake according to directions on packet; pour ¼ cup of the mixture into prepared muffin holes. Pour remaining mixture into pan; bake muffins in moderate oven about 20 minutes and round cake about 40 minutes. Stand cakes in pans 5 minutes; turn onto wire rack to cool. Using serrated knife, level round cake top.

2 Using paper pattern (page 112) from pattern sheet, cut dragon from cake, cut-side down.

3 Place dragon on board, cut-side down. Position muffins for eyes; discard remaining cake.

4 Tint butter cream with pink colouring; spread all over cake.

5 Cut licorice strap into thin strips; position on cake for outline of dragon. Split marshmallow in half horizontally; using a little butter cream, attach one giant red Smartie to each marshmallow half for eyes, position on cake.

6 Cut eyebrows from licorice; position on cake. Position red Smarties on cake for nose; scatter remaining giant Smarties and Smarties on dragon's face.

7 Cut wafers in half on the diagonal; position five pieces on cake for spikes (discard remaining wafer piece). Sprinkle wafers with Twinkle Sprinkles.

Using the paper pattern, cut the dragon's face from the round cake, cut-side down

Place the dragon on the prepared board, cut-side down, then position the muffins for eyes

Place one toothpick at centre of circle and one at the end of each wedge marking

Using the markings as a guide, pipe spider's web onto the top and sides of the cake

Position the steamer cake for spider's body and muffin for spider's head on iced cake

Spoon remaining purple butter cream into piping bag; pipe stars to cover spider's body

creepy crawly spider

cake

5 x 340g packets buttercake mix
40cm-round prepared board (page 112)
5 quantities butter cream (page 112)
green, black and purple colouring

decorations

9 black bump chenille sticks
1 round licorice allsort
1 orange Skittle
5 red Crazy Bananas

1 Preheat oven to moderate. Grease one hole of 12-hole (¹⁄₃ cup/80ml) muffin pan and 1.25-litre (5 cup) pudding steamer; grease and line (page 110) deep 30cm-round cake pan. Make cake according to directions on packet; pour mixture into muffin hole and pudding steamer until each is three-quarters full. Pour remaining mixture into round cake pan; bake muffin in moderate oven about 20 minutes, steamer cake about 45 minutes and round cake about 1 hour. Stand cakes in pans 10 minutes; turn onto wire racks to cool. Using serrated knife, level pudding and round cake tops.

2 Position round cake on board, cut-side down.

3 Tint ³⁄₅ of the butter cream with green colouring; spread all over round cake.

4 Cut 30cm circle from baking paper; fold baking paper into eight equal wedges. Position paper gently on cake; place one toothpick at centre of circle and one toothpick on the outside edge of cake at each wedge marking. Using toothpick, score baking paper from centre of the cake to end of each wedge marking, as shown; remove paper and toothpicks.

5 Tint ¼ of the remaining butter cream with black colouring. Spoon into piping bag (page 115) fitted with 4mm plain tube; using wedge markings as a guide, pipe web on top and side of cake.

6 Position steamer cake for spider body on cake, cut-side down, as shown. Position muffin against body for spider head, as shown.

7 Tint remaining butter cream with purple colouring; spread 2 tablespoons of the purple butter cream over head. Spoon remaining purple butter cream into piping bag (page 115) fitted with a medium fluted tube; pipe stars to cover body, as shown.

8 Bend eight chenille sticks to form spider legs; position on cake. Cut remaining chenille stick into quarters; position two pieces on cake for pincers.

9 Cut allsort in half; position on cake for eyes. Position Skittle on cake for nose and Crazy Bananas for teeth.

you wacky wabbit

cake
3 x 340g packets buttercake mix
38cm x 52cm prepared board (page 112)
3 quantities fluffy frosting (page 114)
black colouring

decorations
icing sugar mixture
200g ready-made soft icing
blue and pink colouring
2 black licorice straps
1 pink marshmallow
6 toothpicks
2 milk bottles
2 black Skittles

1 Preheat oven to moderate; grease and line (page 110) deep 26cm x 36cm baking dish. Make cake according to directions on packet, pour into dish; bake in moderate oven about 1 hour. Stand cake in dish 10 minutes; turn onto wire rack to cool. Using serrated knife, level cake top.

2 Using paper pattern (page 112) from pattern sheet, cut face and outer ears from cake, cut-side down. Assemble cake pieces on board, cut-side down, to form rabbit, as shown; discard remaining cake.

3 Spread ½ of the frosting over lower half of rabbit's face; build up frosting around cheeks to make full. Tint remaining frosting with black colouring to make grey; spread over top half of face and ears of rabbit.

4 On surface dusted with icing sugar, knead icing until smooth; roll ¼ of the icing until 3mm thick. Enclose remaining icing in plastic wrap; reserve. Using paper pattern (page 112) from pattern sheet, cut outer eyes from icing to make whites of eyes; position on cake.

5 On surface dusted with icing sugar, knead blue colouring into ½ of the reserved icing; roll until 3mm thick. Using paper pattern (page 112) from pattern sheet, cut inner eyes (to make irises) and mouth from blue icing; position on cake.

6 On surface dusted with icing sugar, knead pink colouring into remaining icing; roll until 3mm thick. Using paper pattern (page 112) from pattern sheet, cut inner ears from pink icing; position on cake.

7 Cut licorice into thin strips; outline inner ears, eyes and mouth. Position marshmallow for nose.

8 Cut two 10cm, two 9cm and two 8cm pieces from thinly sliced licorice. Pierce one end of each licorice piece with a toothpick; position for whiskers.

9 Trim tops of milk bottles; position for teeth. Position Skittles for eye pupils.

tips Transpose inner ear, mouth, and inner- and outer-eye patterns onto cardboard, then use these templates to cut the shapes from icing.
Be sure to remove toothpicks from cake before cutting and serving.

Place the cake cut-side down then, using paper pattern, cut face and outer ears from cake

Assemble the cake pieces on prepared board, cut-side down, to form the rabbit

Spread the frosting over the lower half of face; build up the frosting around the cheeks

Roll the blue icing until 3mm thick, then cut inner eyes and mouth from icing

friendly flutterby

cake

2 x 340g packets buttercake mix
40cm x 55cm prepared board (page 112)

decorations

icing sugar mixture
1.5kg ready-made soft icing
yellow, green, orange, pink and purple colouring
½ cup (160g) apricot jam, warmed, sieved
2 pink Smarties
2 x 30cm (3mm) yellow chenille sticks (pipe cleaners)

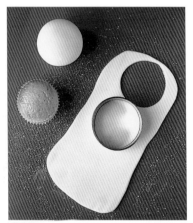

Using 7.5cm-round cutter, cut four rounds from the icing; cover each muffin with one icing round

Using hands dusted with icing sugar, gently mould green icing around each heart cake

Using cutters or a sharp-pointed knife, cut out heart and star shapes from the coloured icings

1 Preheat oven to moderate; grease and line (page 110) two 18cm-heart pans and line four holes of 12-hole (¹/₃ cup/80ml) muffin pan with paper patty cases. Make cake according to directions on packet, place ¼ cup of the cake mixture into each prepared muffin hole and divide remaining cake mixture between heart pans; bake muffins in moderate oven about 20 minutes and heart cakes about 35 minutes. Stand cakes in pans 5 minutes; turn onto wire racks to cool.

2 On surface dusted with icing sugar, knead 350g of the icing until smooth. Knead yellow colouring into icing; roll until 3mm thick. Using 7.5cm-round cutter, cut four rounds from icing; brush tops of muffins with ¼ of the jam, top with rounds of icing. Enclose yellow trimmings in plastic wrap.

3 On surface dusted with icing sugar, knead 500g of the icing until smooth. Knead green colouring into icing; roll until 5mm thick. Brush top and sides of one heart cake with ½ of the remaining jam. Using rolling pin, lift icing over one heart cake; using sharp-pointed knife, neatly trim excess icing at base of cake. Using hands dusted with icing sugar, gently mould icing around heart cake. Repeat with another 500g of the icing, green colouring, jam and remaining heart cake.

4 Assemble icing-covered muffins and cakes on board to form butterfly.

5 On surface dusted with icing sugar, knead remaining icing until smooth. Divide icing into three portions. Knead orange colouring into one portion of the icing; enclose remaining pieces of icing in plastic wrap. Roll orange icing until 3mm thick. Using cutters or sharp-pointed knife, cut heart and star shapes from icing; position on butterfly wings with a little dab of water. Repeat with reserved yellow trimmings and remaining icing portions, one portion tinted pink and one tinted purple.

6 Position Smarties for eyes on butterfly. Using scraps of pink icing, shape a small piece into mouth; position on butterfly.

7 Twist tops of chenille sticks into curls; position on cake for antennae.

up, up and away...
cake

3 x 340g packets buttercake mix
½ cup (160g) apricot jam, warmed, sieved
52cm-round prepared board (page 112)

decorations

icing sugar mixture
pink, green and blue colouring
2.5kg ready-made soft icing
1m (2cm-wide) blue ribbon
1m (2cm-wide) pink ribbon
1m (2cm-wide) green ribbon

1 Preheat oven to moderate; grease and line (page 110) three deep
   20cm-round cake pans. Make cake according to directions on packet,
   divide mixture among pans; bake in moderate oven about 40 minutes.
   Stand cakes in pans 5 minutes; turn onto wire racks to cool.
2 Using small serrated knife, trim cake tops to make more rounded,
   as shown. Brush jam all over cakes.
3 On surface dusted with icing sugar, knead icing until smooth; knead pink
   colouring into ⅓ of the icing. Reserve a walnut-sized amount for balloon
   end; enclose in plastic wrap.
4 Using rolling pin, roll remaining pink icing into circle large enough to cover
   one cake. Using rolling pin, lift icing over one cake; using sharp-pointed
   knife, neatly trim excess icing. Position cake on board.
5 Using hands dusted with icing sugar, gently mould icing into balloon shape.
6 On surface dusted with icing sugar, make balloon end from reserved
   pink icing. Using toothpick or skewer, make creases in balloon end.
   Using toothpick, push end of ribbon into balloon end; attach to cake
   with a tiny dab of water.
7 Repeat with remaining cakes, icing, colourings and ribbons.

*Using a small serrated knife, trim the tops
of the cakes to make more rounded*

*When icing is large enough to cover the cake,
carefully lift icing over cake using a rolling pin*

*Dust your hands with icing sugar then gently
mould the icing into a balloon shape*

*On a surface dusted with icing sugar, mould
the balloon end from the reserved icing*

*Using a toothpick or skewer, make small
creases in the underside of the balloon end*

funny faces

cake

340g packet buttercake mix
1 quantity butter cream (page 112)
yellow, red, green and blue colouring

decorations

1 tablespoon apricot jam, warmed, sieved
icing sugar mixture
250g ready-made soft icing
flesh colouring
cake decorating stars
cake decorating hearts
cake decorating moons
12 assorted coloured mini M&M's
1 quantity piping gel (page 114)
black colouring

1 Preheat oven to moderate; line six holes of 12-hole (⅓ cup/80ml) muffin pan with paper patty cases. Make cake according to directions on packet, pour ¼ cup mixture into each hole; bake in moderate oven about 20 minutes. Stand cakes in pan 5 minutes; turn onto wire rack to cool.

2 Divide butter cream into quarters; tint ¼ with yellow colouring, ¼ with red colouring, ¼ with green colouring and ¼ with blue colouring.

3 Brush tops of cakes with jam. On surface dusted with icing sugar, knead icing until smooth. Knead flesh colouring into icing; roll icing until 3mm thick. Using 7.5cm round cutter, cut six rounds from icing; cover each patty cake with one round.

4 Place yellow butter cream into piping bag (page 115) fitted with a fluted tube; pipe random hairstyles onto one or two patty cakes. Repeat with red, green and blue butter creams, cleaning or replacing piping bag between colours.

5 Decorate hairstyles with stars, hearts and moons. Position M&M's on each cake for eyes; secure with tiny dabs of butter cream.

6 Tint ½ of the piping gel with red colouring; tint remaining piping gel with black colouring. Place piping gels in separate paper piping bags (page 115). Using piping gels, pipe pupils, eyebrows, noses, freckles, mouths, eyelashes, ears and glasses onto cakes, as desired.

tips Use extra mini M&M's for ears, earrings, etc, if desired.
The cake mix is enough to make 12 patty cakes, so decorate the other six patty cakes into other family or classmate faces.

king of pops

cake

2 x 340g packets buttercake mix
30cm-round prepared board (page 112)
1 jam rollette
1 bamboo skewer
2 quantities butter cream (page 112)
burgundy colouring

decorations

32 boiled lollies
5 heart-shaped lollipops
15g packet silver cachous
2 x 15cm (6mm) silver glitter chenille sticks (pipe cleaners)
8 x 30cm (6mm) silver glitter chenille sticks (pipe cleaners)

Cut one of the cakes in half, then cut one of the halves in half again to make two quarters

1 Preheat oven to moderate; grease and line (page 110) two deep 20cm-round cake pans. Make cake according to directions on packet, divide mixture between pans; bake in moderate oven about 40 minutes. Stand cakes in pans 5 minutes; turn onto wire racks to cool. Using serrated knife, level cake tops so cakes are the same height.

2 Cut one cake in half; cut one of the halves in half again, as shown. Trim and discard a 2cm slice from each of the two cake quarters, as shown.

3 Place whole cake on board, cut-side down; sit half-cake, on its side, across centre of whole cake. Place trimmed cake quarters opposite each other on either side of half-cake. Trim and discard about 1cm from rollette, position on top of crown; secure with skewer. Discard remaining cake.

4 Tint butter cream with burgundy colouring; spread all over crown.

5 Decorate cake with boiled lollies, lollipops and cachous. Bend 15cm chenille sticks to form semi-circles; position gently into top of crown. Bend 30cm chenille sticks to form semi-circles; position around side of crown.

Assemble the cake pieces on the board, secure the trimmed rollette with the bamboo skewer

Place the cakes together at short edges then, using the paper pattern, cut out the rainbow

Assemble the cake pieces on the board then, using a serrated knife, trim edges on an angle

Carefully pipe coloured sugars along the rainbow; each colour should be about 1.5cm wide

rainbow's end

cake

6 x 340g packets buttercake mix
62cm x 82cm prepared board (page 112)
2½ quantities butter cream (page 112)
yellow colouring

decorations

1.1kg (5¼ cups) white sugar
purple, blue, green, yellow, orange and pink colouring
artificial spider's web

1. Preheat oven to moderate; grease and line (page 110) two deep 26cm x 36cm baking dishes. Make cake according to directions on packet, divide mixture between dishes; bake in moderate oven about 1 hour. Stand cakes in dishes 10 minutes; turn onto wire rack to cool. Using serrated knife, level cake tops so cakes are the same height.
2. Place cakes together at short edges; using paper pattern (page 112) from pattern sheet, cut rainbow from cakes, cut-side down, as shown.
3. Assemble cakes on board, cut-side down, to form rainbow; discard remaining cake. Using serrated knife, trim ends of rainbow at an angle, as shown.
4. Tint butter cream with yellow colouring; spread all over rainbow.
5. Place 1½ cups (330g) of the sugar and purple colouring in small plastic bag; rub purple colouring into sugar until evenly coloured. Place ½ of the sugar in piping bag (page 115). Cut tip off piping bag to 5mm diameter. Starting from inside the circle of the rainbow, carefully pipe sugar along rainbow.
6. Place some extra purple colouring into the same plastic bag with remaining sugar; rub until sugar is evenly coloured to make deeper purple. Place in piping bag; carefully pipe sugar along rainbow.
7. Place ¾ cup (165g) of the sugar and blue colouring in small plastic bag; rub blue colouring into sugar until evenly coloured. Place sugar in piping bag; carefully pipe sugar along rainbow. Repeat with remaining sugar and green, yellow, orange and pink colouring.
8. Decorate rainbow with spider's web for clouds.

Using the paper pattern, cut the popcorn and the box from the cake, cut-side down

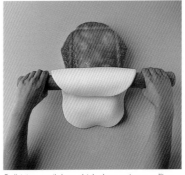

Roll icing until 1cm thick then, using a rolling pin, carefully place the icing over the box

Mould icing over the box then cut across the top of icing to make the top edge of the box

Place evenly-spaced 26cm strips vertically on the front of the box then trim excess icing

pop star

cake

3 x 340g packets buttercake mix
35cm x 45cm prepared board (page 112)

decorations

⅓ cup (110g) apricot jam, warmed, sieved
icing sugar mixture
1.3kg ready-made soft icing
red colouring
½ quantity butter cream (page 112)
1½ cups (40g) coloured popcorn
1½ cups (20g) buttered popcorn

1 Preheat oven to moderate; grease and line (page 110) deep 26cm x 36cm baking dish. Make cake according to directions on packet, pour into dish; bake in moderate oven about 1 hour. Stand cake in dish 10 minutes; turn onto wire rack to cool. Using serrated knife, level cake top.

2 Using paper pattern (page 112) from pattern sheet, cut popcorn and box from cake. Place on board, cut-side down; discard remaining cake. Brush ¾ of the jam over box.

3 On surface dusted with icing sugar, knead 1kg of the icing until smooth; roll until 1cm thick. Using rolling pin, carefully place icing over box.

4 Using hands dusted with icing sugar, gently mould icing over box; cut across top of icing to make top edge of box. Trim excess icing from sides of box.

5 On surface dusted with icing sugar, knead remaining icing until smooth. Knead red colouring into icing; roll until 5mm thick. Cut one 1.5cm x 31cm strip and six 1.5cm x 26cm strips from icing; working with one strip at a time, brush remaining jam onto underside of each strip.

6 Place the 31cm strip along top edge of popcorn box; place evenly-spaced 26cm strips vertically on front of popcorn box, as shown. Trim away excess icing from each strip. Cover uniced cake with butter cream; cover with combined coloured and buttered popcorn.

the ghostly galleon

cake

3 x 340g packets buttercake mix
25cm x 40cm prepared board (page 112)
8 skewers
3 quantities butter cream (page 112)
black colouring

decorations

9 x 25g packets Curly Wurly
24 Crazy Bananas
12 white Life Savers
15g milk chocolate block
3 x 10cm-square pieces white cardboard
3 x 8cm-square pieces white cardboard
6.5cm x 8.5cm Jolly Roger picture (see pattern sheet)

Cut the cake in half lengthways, then cut a 7cm piece from each of the two halves

Assemble the cake pieces on the board to form the galleon, then secure with five skewers

Trim the front of the galleon at angles, then trim skewers to the same height as the cake

1 Preheat oven to moderate; grease and line (page 110) deep 26cm x 36cm baking dish. Make cake according to directions on packet, pour into pan; bake in moderate oven about 1 hour. Stand cake in pan 10 minutes; turn onto wire rack to cool. Using serrated knife, level cake top.

2 Cut cake in half lengthways, cut-side down; cut 7cm piece from each half, as shown.

3 Assemble cake pieces on board to form galleon, as shown; secure with five skewers.

4 Trim front of galleon at angles to make bow, as shown; discard cake trimmings. Trim skewers to the same height as the cake.

5 Tint butter cream with black colouring; spread all over galleon.

6 Decorate galleon with pieces of Curly Wurly, as shown.

7 Decorate galleon with Crazy Bananas and Life Savers. Position chocolate for plank; support by placing piece of skewer or toothpick underneath.

8 Thread large then small cardboard pieces on remaining skewers. Photocopy Jolly Roger picture from pattern sheet; position at top of centre skewer. Position the three masts on galleon.

tips If the Curly Wurly will not stay in place, secure them with toothpicks. You may need to place two pieces of Curly Wurly side-by-side in order to get the desired length.

Be sure to remove skewers before cutting and serving cake.

60

lamington choo choo

cake

8 x 6cm-square (3.5cm-deep) ready-made lamingtons
40cm x 50cm prepared board (page 112)

decorations

3 green Fruit Sticks, halved
4 x 20g packets Five Flavours Life Savers
2 x 400g packets jelly beans

1 Place one lamington at front of board. Cut ⅓ from another lamington; position larger lamington piece in front of whole lamington for train's engine. Completely hollow out smaller lamington piece; top whole lamington with hollowed lamington piece.

2 Using small serrated knife, cut shallow hollows into remaining lamingtons.

3 Connect six lamingtons, hollow-side up, to train's engine with Fruit Sticks, to make train's carriages.

4 Position two Life Savers on top of engine; position remaining Life Savers on each carriage for wheels.

5 Stand two jelly beans in Life Savers on engine; place three black jelly beans at front of engine. Fill each carriage and hollow of engine with remaining jelly beans.

Place larger piece on board for engine then hollow out the smaller piece of the lamington

Top the whole lamington with the hollowed smaller piece to make the front of the train

Using a small serrated knife, cut shallow hollows into the remaining lamingtons

Brush cut-side of each cake with some jam, then join the cut-sides to make a sphere

Using hands dusted with icing sugar, rub the icing to cover the head and make smooth

Insert a toothpick into each Psychedelic Snake then press them into the head for hair

Shape the remaining icing into eyebrows and lips, then place the teeth lolly in position

Cut the remaining green jube into small triangles, then position on face for eyelashes

psycho-deliah

cake

3 x 340g packets buttercake mix
½ cup (160g) apricot jam, warmed, sieved
30cm-round prepared board (page 112)

decorations

icing sugar mixture
1.5kg ready-made soft icing
flesh and red colouring
1 black Super Rope licorice
100 wooden toothpicks, with double-pointed ends
4 x 200g packets Psychedelic Snakes Alive
1 large teeth lolly
2 green jubes
2 giant purple Smarties
2 mini red M&M's
26 silver cachous
1 black licorice strap
2 blue cachous

1 Preheat oven to moderate; grease two 1.75-litre (7 cup) pudding steamers. Make cake according to directions on packet, divide mixture between steamers; bake in moderate oven about 50 minutes. Stand cakes in steamers 5 minutes; turn onto wire rack to cool. Using serrated knife, level cake tops.

2 Brush cut-side of cakes with some of the jam; join cut-sides together to make head. Position head on board; brush with remaining jam.

3 On surface dusted with icing sugar, knead icing until smooth. Knead flesh colouring into icing; roll 1.25kg of the icing until 5mm thick, and enclose remaining icing in plastic wrap. Using rolling pin, carefully lift icing over head. Using hands dusted with icing sugar, mould icing to completely cover head; rub icing gently with hands to smooth.

4 Trim Super Rope for collar to fit around base of head. Secure collar to head with a toothpick.

5 Insert a toothpick into one end of each Psychedelic Snake; press into head for hair. Use shorter Snakes at front for fringe.

6 Place about 1 teaspoon of the reserved icing in a cup; stir in a drop or two of warm water to make a thick paste. Cover paste; reserve.

7 Using hands dusted with icing sugar, shape remaining icing into eyebrows and lips. Trim gum of teeth lolly to fit into lips. Brush or dab a little of the reserved paste onto the back of the mouth and eyebrows; position on head.

8 Using paste, position one jube on face for nose, Smarties under brows for eyes and M&M's on Smarties for pupils.

9 Cut remaining jube into triangles; position on face with paste for eyelashes.

10 Using paste, attach silver cachous to collar. Cut small piece from licorice strap for eyebrow ring; position on cake. Using paste, attach one blue cachou on eyebrow ring. Using paste, attach blue cachou to nose for nose ring. Using red colouring and small paintbrush, paint eyebrows and lips, then freckles on cheeks.

tip Be sure to remove all toothpicks from cake before cutting.

françois ze frog

cake

3 x 340g packets buttercake mix
40cm-square prepared board (page 112)
2 quantities butter cream (page 112)
green and red colouring

decorations

14 brown Smarties
2 red Smarties
18 red frogs
18 green frogs
1 green and yellow bow

1. Preheat oven to moderate; grease and line (page 110) deep 26cm x 36cm baking dish. Make cake according to directions on packet, pour into pan; bake in moderate oven about 1 hour. Stand cake in pan 10 minutes; turn onto wire rack to cool. Using serrated knife, level cake top.

2. Using paper pattern (page 112) from pattern sheet, cut frog's body and eyes from cake, cut-side down.

3. Assemble cake pieces on board, cut-side down, to form frog; discard remaining cake.

4. Reserve 2 tablespoons of the butter cream for eyes. Tint ¾ of the remaining butter cream with green colouring; tint remaining butter cream with red colouring. Spread green butter cream all over cake.

5. Carefully place paper pattern on cake for eyes, face and front legs; using toothpick, mark outline on cake.

6. Spoon red butter cream into piping bag (page 115) fitted with 4mm plain tube; pipe over marked outlines and around edge of frog. Pipe smile on face.

7. Spread reserved plain butter cream on eyes; position brown Smarties for pupils and toes. Position red Smarties for nose. Position red and green frogs around side of cake; position bow under frog's chin.

Using the paper pattern, cut the frog's body and eyes from the cake, cut-side down

Assemble the cake pieces on board, cut-side down, to form frog; discard remaining cake

Place patterns on cake for eyes, face and front legs; using a toothpick, mark outline on cake

Place the butter cream into a piping bag; pipe over marked outlines and around edge of frog

castle of darkness

cake

3 x 340g packets buttercake mix
30cm-round prepared board
   (page 112)
2 quantities butter cream (page 112)
purple colouring
2 jam rollettes

decorations

1 bamboo skewer
8cm-round black cardboard
6 mint sticks
150g white chocolate Melts, melted
yellow colouring
100g milk chocolate Melts, melted
27 sections dark chocolate
   Toblerone (approximately
   3 x 100g bars)
artificial spider's web

1 Preheat oven to moderate; grease and line (page 110) deep 13cm-round cake pan and two deep 20cm-round cake pans. Make cake according to directions on packet, pour mixture into 13cm pan until three-quarters full. Divide remaining mixture between 20cm pans; bake 13cm cake in moderate oven about 35 minutes and 20cm cakes about 40 minutes. Stand cakes in pans 5 minutes; turn onto wire racks to cool. Using serrated knife, level cake tops.

2 Place one 20cm cake on board, cut-side up. Tint butter cream with purple colouring; spread cake top with ½ cup of the butter cream. Top cake with remaining 20cm cake, cut-side down.

3 Spread cut-side of 13cm cake with ¼ cup of butter cream; centre, butter-cream down, on 20cm cake stack.

4 Position rollettes on top of stacked cakes; secure with skewer, as shown. Spread remaining butter cream all over cakes.

5 Cut slit from edge to centre of cardboard round; roll cardboard into cone shape, as shown. Secure with sticky tape on inside of cone; position cone on cake top.

6 Position mint sticks together on bottom of cake for door.

7 Draw five 3cm x 5.5cm and seven 2cm x 3cm windows on sheet of baking paper. Tint white chocolate with yellow colouring; place in piping bag (page 115). Pipe windows onto baking paper; stand until chocolate sets.

8 Place milk chocolate in separate piping bag. Pipe spiders onto sheet of baking paper; stand until chocolate sets.

9 Decorate castle with windows, spiders, Toblerone and spider's web.

Place one 20cm cake on the board then spread the cut side with ½ cup of the butter cream

Stack the jam rollettes on the cake then secure them with a skewer to make a tower

Cut a small slit from the edge to centre of the cardboard round, then roll it to form a cone

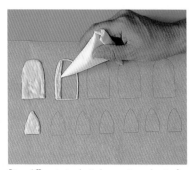
Pipe different-sized windows onto a sheet of baking paper, then stand until set

Using milk chocolate, pipe the spiders onto a sheet of baking paper, then stand until set

sam the tool man

cake

2 x 340g packets buttercake mix
45cm-square prepared board (page 112)

decorations

icing sugar mixture
200g ready-made soft icing
1 quantity butter cream
blue colouring
yellow colouring
candy cake decorations (page 115)
assorted toy tools

1 Preheat oven to moderate; grease 1.75-litre (7 cup) pudding steamer.
   Make cake according to directions on packet, pour into steamer until
   three-quarters full; bake in moderate oven about 50 minutes. Stand cake
   in steamer 5 minutes; turn onto wire rack to cool. Using serrated knife,
   level cake top.
2 Place cake on board, cut-side down.
3 On surface dusted with icing sugar, knead icing until smooth; roll ½ of
   the icing until 3mm thick. Cut hat peak from icing; mould around cake.
4 Tint butter cream with blue colouring; spread all over cake and peak.
5 Knead yellow colouring into remaining icing; roll ¾ of the icing into
   thick cord. Position around edge of hat.
6 Roll remaining icing until 3mm thick; cut out name plaque. Position name
   and desired candy cake decorations on plaque using a little water; position
   plaque on hat.
7 Place assorted toy tools around cake on board.

tip Make patty cakes from any leftover cake mixture.

Cut the hat's peak from the plain icing then mould it around the front edge of the cake

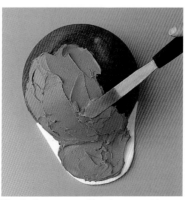
Tint the butter cream blue then spread it over the cake and peak with a palette knife

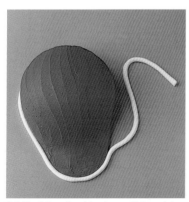
Roll ¾ of the yellow icing into a thick cord then position the cord around the edge of the hat

fifi the poodle

You need approximately 4 x 150g packets of mallow bakes.

cake
3 x 340g packets buttercake mix
46cm x 50cm prepared board (page 112)
2 quantities butter cream (page 112)
pink colouring

decorations
6 black licorice twists
200g white mallow bakes
275g white marshmallows
1 black licorice strap

Using the paper pattern, cut poodle's body, feet and tail from the cake, cut-side down

Assemble the cake pieces on the prepared board, cut-side down, to form the poodle

1 Preheat oven to moderate; grease and line (page 110) deep 26cm x 36cm baking dish. Make cake according to directions on packet, pour into pan; bake in moderate oven about 1 hour. Stand cake in pan 10 minutes; turn onto wire rack to cool. Using serrated knife, level cake top.

2 Using paper pattern (page 112) from pattern sheet, cut poodle's body, feet and tail from cake, cut-side down.

3 Assemble cake pieces on board, cut-side down, to form poodle; discard remaining cake.

4 Tint butter cream with pink colouring; spread all over cake.

5 Trim one licorice twist to 11cm; position on cake for tail. Trim another licorice twist to 8cm; position on cake for ear. Trim remaining licorice twists to 8cm; position on cake for legs.

6 Decorate body and feet with mallow bakes. Decorate head, ear and tail with marshmallows.

7 Cut licorice strap into thin strips, position around outline of poodle face; cut shorter pieces for eye and mouth. Trim 5mm piece from licorice twist trimmings; position on cake for nose.

tip If you find that the marshmallows don't sit in place firmly when decorating the ear, secure them with toothpicks, but be sure to remove them before serving.

play pool
cake

2 x 340g packets buttercake mix
35cm-round prepared board (page 112)

decorations

85g packet bubblegum-flavoured jelly crystals
½ cup (160g) apricot jam, warmed, sieved
icing sugar mixture
1kg ready-made soft icing
purple, green, yellow, pink and blue colouring
2 toy dolls

Using the markings as a guide, cut a shallow hollow from the cake with a serrated knife

1 Preheat oven to moderate; grease and line (page 110) deep 22cm-round cake pan. Make cake according to directions on packet, pour into pan; bake in moderate oven about 50 minutes. Stand cake in pan 5 minutes; turn onto wire rack to cool. Using serrated knife, level cake top.

2 Make jelly according to manufacturer's instructions; refrigerate until almost set.

3 Position cake on board, cut-side down. Using ruler and toothpicks, mark a 19cm circle in centre of cake. Using markings as a guide and small serrated knife, cut 2cm-deep hollow from cake. Brush top edge and side of cake with jam.

Roll the icing into a rope long enough to reach around the circumference of the cake

4 On surface dusted with icing sugar, knead icing until smooth. Knead purple colouring into 200g of the icing; roll ¾ of the purple icing into a rope long enough to reach around the bottom circumference of cake. Enclose remaining purple icing in plastic wrap; reserve. Position rope around cake. Repeat with 200g batches of icing and green, yellow and pink colouring, stacking the coloured ropes up the outside of the cake.

5 Knead blue colouring into remaining white icing; roll ½ of the icing into a rope long enough to reach around the top edge of the cake. Flatten rope slightly with rolling pin; position on cake for top of pool. Roll remaining blue icing into a rope long enough to reach around the circumference of the cake; position on cake above pink rope.

Shape half of the blue icing around the top edge of the play pool

6 When jelly is almost set, stir gently to break up; spoon into hollowed section of cake. Position dolls in pool.

7 On surface dusted with icing sugar, shape reserved icings into pool toys; position in and around pool just before serving.

tip It's important not to position the pool toys in the pool until just before serving the cake, because they will dissolve soon after they touch the jelly.

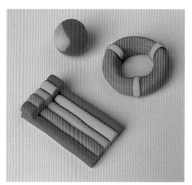

Shape the reserved icings into pool toys, but don't position in the pool until serving the cake

girlie ghost

cake

2 x 340g packets buttercake mix
40cm-round prepared board (page 112)
1 quantity butter cream (page 112)
blue colouring

decorations

icing sugar mixture
1.2kg ready-made soft icing
purple bow

1 Preheat oven to moderate; grease Dolly Varden pan. Make cake according to directions on packet, pour mixture into pan until three-quarters full; bake in moderate oven about 1 hour. Stand cake in pan 5 minutes; turn onto wire rack to cool. Using serrated knife, level cake top.
2 Place cake on board, cut-side down.
3 Tint butter cream with blue colouring; spread all over cake.
4 On surface dusted with icing sugar, knead icing until smooth; roll icing into 5mm-thick circle large enough to generously cover cake. Using metal cutters or small sharp-pointed knife, cut eyes and mouth near centre of icing circle. Using rolling pin, lift icing over cake, draping so eyes and mouth are positioned in the right spot. Icing will stretch slightly as it is lifted over the cake. Trim draped icing on board to neaten shape of ghost.
5 Using a little butter cream, secure bow to cake.

tip You can make patty cakes with any leftover cake mixture.

Tint the butter cream with blue colouring then, using a palette knife, spread it all over the cake

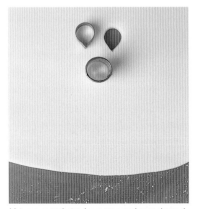

Using a metal circular cutter and tear-shaped cutter, cut the eyes and mouth from the icing

howdy sheriff

cake
3 x 340g packets buttercake mix
35cm-square prepared board (page 112)
2 quantities butter cream (page 112)
yellow and red colouring

decorations
6 chocolate freckles
42 silver cachous

1 Preheat oven to moderate; grease and line (page 110) deep 30cm-square cake pan. Make cake according to directions on packet, pour into pan; bake in moderate oven about 1 hour 15 minutes. Stand cake in pan 10 minutes; turn onto wire rack to cool. Using serrated knife, level cake top.

2 Using paper pattern (page 112) from pattern sheet, cut badge from cake, cut-side down. Place on board, cut-side down; discard remaining cake.

3 Tint ⅔ of the butter cream with yellow colouring; spread all over cake.

4 Tint remaining butter cream with red colouring; spoon into piping bag (page 115) fitted with 4mm plain tube; pipe ½ of the red butter cream around edges of badge.

5 Position freckles on badge. Using tweezers, decorate cake with cachous.

6 Pipe name onto cake with remaining red butter cream.

Using the paper pattern, cut sheriff's badge from the square cake, cut-side down

Using a piping bag fitted with a 4mm plain tube, pipe around the edges of sheriff's badge

Pipe the birthday child's name onto sheriff's badge with the remaining red butter cream

Assemble cakes, jam rolls and rollettes, and staircase to make castle

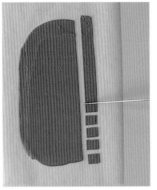

Spread pink chocolate onto baking paper; when almost set, cut into tiles

Overlap chocolate tiles to cover roofs of towers; use pointed piece for each spire

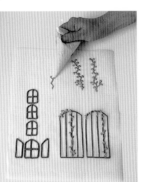

Pipe windows, window shutters, gates and vines onto baking paper

palace of dreams

This cake is not difficult — it is, however, time consuming.

cake

4 x 340g packets buttercake mix
36cm x 46cm prepared board (page 112)
2 x 400g jam rolls
250g packet jam rollettes
bamboo skewers
2 Sherbert Cones
6 quantities butter cream (page 112)
purple, green and pink colouring

decorations

¼ cup (60g) Twinkle Sprinkles
2 teaspoons vegetable oil
250g white chocolate Melts, melted
60 Sherbet Fizzes
10 blue boiled lollies
4 coloured Fruit Sticks
7 coloured marshmallows
assorted mini fairies and frog

1 Preheat oven to moderate; grease and line (page 110) deep 19cm-square cake pan and deep 26cm x 36cm baking dish. Make cake according to directions on packet, pour ¼ of the mixture into square pan and remaining mixture into baking dish; bake square cake in moderate oven about 30 minutes and cake in baking dish about 1 hour. Stand cakes 10 minutes; turn onto wire racks to cool. Using serrated knife, level cake tops.

2 Place large cake on board, cut-side down. Cut 3 steps for staircase from one short side of cake. Place square cake on bench, cut-side down; cut 4cm x 6cm piece out of one corner. Cut 3 steps into this piece. Position square cake so cut-out section is at the back of cake; position stairs on large cake.

3 Position jam rolls and rollettes for towers. Using small serrated knife, shape tops of three towers. Position tallest tower where square cake was cut. Position remaining towers on cake; secure with skewers.

4 Discard filling from Sherbet Cones.

5 Tint ½ of the butter cream purple, ⅔ of remaining butter cream green and remaining butter cream pink.

6 Place ⅓ of the purple butter cream in small bowl, tint a deeper purple; spread over stairs and top of square cake. Spread centre tower with pink butter cream. Spread remaining purple butter cream over remaining towers, Sherbert Cones and sides of square cake. Roll Sherbert Cones in ½ of the Twinkle Sprinkles; position Sherbert Cones on front towers. Spread green butter cream over top and sides of large cake.

7 Stir oil into melted chocolate; tint ⅖ of the chocolate pink. Spread over baking paper; stand until almost set. Cut into 1.5cm x 2cm tiles. Position on roofs of two towers. Cut two tiles into pointed pieces; position for spires.

8 Tint ⅔ of remaining melted chocolate purple. Using ½ of purple chocolate, make tiles and a spire; position on third tower. Reserve remaining purple chocolate.

9 Draw three 2.5cm x 3cm windows, one 3cm x 4cm window, two 1.5cm x 4cm window shutters and two 5cm x 10cm gates on baking paper. Pipe reserved purple chocolate over tracings; stand until set.

10 Tint remaining melted chocolate green. Pipe vines on gates and a few smaller vines on baking paper; stand until set.

11 Position windows, window shutters, gates and vines on castle; use Sherbet Fizzes to outline garden.

12 Place boiled lollies in plastic bag; use rolling pin or meat mallet to crush coarsely. Use for ponds.

13 Make mushrooms using Fruit Sticks for stems and marshmallows for caps; place mushrooms around castle. Brush tops of mushrooms with a little water; sprinkle lightly with some of the Twinkle Sprinkles.

14 Scatter more Twinkle Sprinkles around castle.

tip Be sure to remove skewers before cutting and serving cake.

80

fairy godmother

cake

2 x 340g packets buttercake mix
20cm-round thick cardboard
1 quantity butter cream (page 112)
white colouring

decorations

28cm doll
50cm white sheer organza
50cm silver glitter fabric
1m white tulle
white cotton thread
silver glitter pen
1m silver twine with stars
craft glue
8cm (6mm) silver glitter chenille stick (pipe cleaner)
20cm diamante chain
6cm x 12cm white faux fur
1.5cm x 50cm silver ribbon

Place cake, cut-side down, on cardboard on bowl, then gently push the doll into the cake

1 Preheat oven to moderate. Grease Dolly Varden pan. Make cake according to directions on packet, pour mixture into prepared pan until three-quarters full; bake in moderate oven about 1 hour. Stand cake in pan 5 minutes; turn onto wire rack to cool. Using serrated knife, level cake top.

2 Cover cardboard with grease-proof paper or foil (page 112). Using sharp knife, cut 10cm circle from centre of cardboard for doll's feet to protrude through. Stand cardboard on saucer or wide shallow bowl, top-side up, to support the cake. Place cake on cardboard circle, cut-side down.

3 Gently push doll down into cake through centre to waist level; remove doll.

4 Tint butter cream with white colouring; spread all over cake.

5 Cut one 42cm circle from organza and one from glitter fabric; cut two 42cm circles from tulle. Cut 4.5cm-round hole in centre of organza and glitter fabric circles; cut 4.5cm-round hole in centre of one tulle circle.

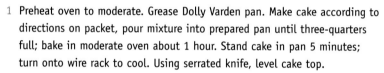

Decorate the edges of all fabric circles and wings with the glitter pen; stand until the glitter sets

6 To make wings: Using paper pattern (page 112) from pattern sheet, cut sections from tulle circle without the hole. Gather long opposing edges together; secure by wrapping cotton thread tightly around centre gather. Decorate edges of all fabric circles and wings with glitter pen; stand until glitter sets.

7 Cut stars from 85cm of the twine; using glue, position one star on chenille stick for wand, and remaining stars on wings and ¼ of the organza circle, to make front panel of skirt.

8 Place tulle circle over cake; top with organza circle, positioning stars to the front. Top with glitter fabric. Gather front edge of the glitter fabric up, as shown; stitch to secure. Glue 1cm of diamante chain over gather.

9 Cut bodice for doll from fur; glue into position. Use diamante chain to make bracelet and necklace; secure with cotton thread. Glue wand to doll's hand.

10 Twist remaining twine into tiara shape; twist ends together under hair to hold in place. Push doll carefully into cake to waist level, as shown.

11 Glue wings onto doll. Tie ribbon around waist to cover top of skirt.

After decorating the upper half of the doll, gently push the doll into the decorated cake

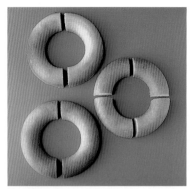

Place the cakes, cut-side down, then cut cakes into segments with a small serrated knife

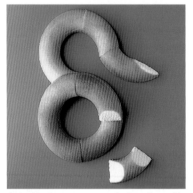

Assemble the segments on the board, cut-side down, then trim the tail piece on the diagonal

Using a rolling pin, roll mallow bakes to flatten then divide them into groups by their colour

snake, rattle and roll

This cake is not at all difficult, however it is time consuming. You can flatten the mallow bakes up to a day ahead; be sure to store them in an airtight container.

cake

2 x 340g packets buttercake mix
43cm x 45cm prepared board (page 112)
2 quantities butter cream (page 112)
yellow colouring

decorations

5 x 100g packets rainbow mallow bakes
2 strawberries & creams
1 red snake

1 Preheat oven to moderate; grease three 22cm savarin tins. Make cake according to directions on packet, divide mixture among tins; bake in moderate oven about 25 minutes. Stand cakes in tins 5 minutes; turn onto wire racks to cool. Using serrated knife, level cake tops so cakes are the same height.

2 Cut cakes into segments, as shown. Assemble segments on board, cut-side down, to form snake. Cut both ends of one cake-quarter on the diagonal for head. Trim end piece of snake on the diagonal for tail; discard remaining cake.

3 Using rolling pin, flatten mallow bakes; divide mallow bakes by colour.

4 Tint butter cream with yellow colouring. Starting at tail of snake, spread butter cream over segment; cover with slightly overlapping mallow bakes.

5 Continue working in segments, connecting each segment with butter cream.

6 Attach snake's head to body with butter cream; spread remaining butter cream over head.

7 Position strawberries & creams for eyes; position red snake for tongue.

tip Savarin tins are available at cookware shops. If you only have one savarin tin, pour ⅓ of the cake mixture into the tin and bake it according to the recipe. The cake mixture will be fine if you can only bake one cake at a time.

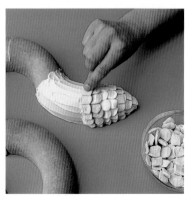

Starting at the tail end, cover a segment with butter cream then with coloured mallow bakes

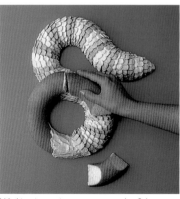

Working in sections, connect each of the segments with a little of the butter cream

Attach the snake's head to the body with butter cream then continue with mallow bakes

zappo the alien

You need one 200g packet of Skittles.

cake

2 x 340g packets buttercake mix
30cm x 46cm prepared board (page 112)
2 quantities butter cream (page 112)
green colouring

decorations

2 yellow Skittles
2 giant Jaffas
27 green Skittles
1 red fruit ring
rainbow choc-chips
2 green lollipops
7 spearmint leaves
7 toothpicks
12 orange Cool Fruits
9 yellow Cool Fruits

Assemble the cooled cakes on the prepared board, top-side up

Spread green butter cream over the top and sides of the cakes with a palette knife

1 Preheat oven to moderate; grease and line (page 110) deep 20cm-round cake pan and deep 18cm-oval cake pan. Make cake according to directions on packet, divide mixture between pans so that both mixtures are to the same depth; bake round cake in moderate oven about 35 minutes and oval cake about 40 minutes. Stand cakes in pans 5 minutes; turn onto wire rack to cool.

2 Assemble cakes on board, as shown.

3 Tint butter cream with green colouring; use a little butter cream to attach oval cake to round cake. Spread remaining butter cream all over cakes.

4 Attach yellow Skittles to Jaffas with a little butter cream for eyes; position on cake. Position 1 green Skittle for nose; position fruit ring for mouth. Sprinkle rainbow choc-chips on cheeks and top of head; position lollipops on head for antennae.

5 Skewer each spearmint leaf with a toothpick; position on sides and top of head. Scatter Cool Fruits and remaining green Skittles on body of alien.

merry-go-round

This cake is not difficult – it is, however, time consuming.

cake
3 x 340g packets buttercake mix
33cm-round prepared board (page 112)

decorations
cardboard cylinder
16 x 20cm (6mm-wide) assorted coloured ribbons
8 x 25cm-long thick bamboo skewers, trimmed to 20cm
8 x 18cm (6mm-wide) assorted coloured ribbons
8 small unpainted craftwood horses
¼ cup (80g) apricot jam, warmed, sieved
icing sugar mixture
1.5kg ready-made soft icing
pink colouring
22cm-round thick cardboard
1 egg white
1½ cups (240g) pure icing sugar
2 x 250g packets Fruit Sticks
2 x 15g packets Fizzers
glue gun
2 x 15g packets coloured cachous

Wrap two 20cm ribbons around each skewer then secure with tape

Score baking paper and icing with a toothpick to make eight markings

Position one ribbon-wrapped skewer into each toothpick marking

Carefully centre the shallow cake on skewers and cardboard cylinder

1 Preheat oven to moderate; grease one hole of 6-hole Texas (¾ cup/180ml) muffin pan, and grease and line (page 110) two deep 22cm-round cake pans. Make cake according to directions on packet, pour ⅓ of the mixture into one round pan, ½ cup mixture into prepared muffin hole and remaining mixture into other round pan. Bake muffin in moderate oven about 25 minutes, shallow cake about 40 minutes and deep cake about 55 minutes. Stand cakes in pans 5 minutes; turn onto wire racks to cool. Using serrated knife, level top of deep cake.

2 Trim cardboard cylinder to 20cm. Using sticky tape, secure two 20cm ribbons to one end of a skewer; wrap ribbon around skewer, as shown. Secure other end with tape. Repeat with remaining 20cm ribbons and skewers. Tie 18cm ribbons around necks of horses.

3 Brush cakes all over with jam. On surface dusted with icing sugar mixture, knead icing until smooth. Knead pink colouring into icing; roll ½ of the icing until large enough to cover deep cake. Enclose remaining icing in plastic wrap; reserve.

4 Using rolling pin, place icing over cake; trim around base of cake. Position cake on board. Roll ¾ of the reserved icing until large enough to cover shallow cake. Using rolling pin, place icing over cake; trim around base of cake. Position shallow cake on cardboard round. Roll remaining

icing until large enough to cover muffin. Using rolling pin, place icing over muffin; trim around base of muffin.

5 Cut 22cm circle from baking paper; fold baking paper into eight equal wedges. Position paper on deep cake; using toothpick, score paper through to icing on wedge-shaped tracings, alternately at 1.5cm and 5cm points from outside edge of cake, as shown. Discard paper.

6 Push cardboard cylinder through the centre of the deep cake to the board. Insert one ribbon-wrapped skewer into each toothpick marking, making sure the skewers and cardboard cylinder are of the same height.

7 Stir egg white and sifted pure icing sugar together in small bowl until smooth. Brush cardboard cylinder all over with egg mixture; position 14 Fruit Sticks upright against cylinder. Decorate top of cylinder with Fizzers.

8 Centre muffin on top of shallow cake; carefully centre shallow cake on top of skewers and cylinder. Using glue gun, secure one horse to each skewer.

9 Using egg mixture, decorate carousel with remaining Fruit Sticks and cachous. Use Fruit Stick trimmings to make stars; position on cake using egg mixture.

tips We painted the horses with non-toxic paint. The cardboard cylinder must be strong – we used the inside of a baking paper roll.

88

little cakes of horror

cake

340g packet buttercake mix
1½ quantities butter cream
  (page 112)
green, red, black and
  blue colouring

decorations

SNAKES

7 Brite Crawlers
black glossy decorating gel

EYEBALL

1 large white marshmallow
1 giant black Smartie
white glossy decorating gel

BAT

1 black jelly bean
1 black licorice strap
white glossy decorating gel
black glossy decorating gel
3 white cake decorating stars

GHOSTS

2 milk bottles
black glossy decorating gel

CAT

1 giant brown Smartie
1 brown Smartie
1 black licorice strap
1 yellow Crazy Banana
3 yellow cake decorating stars
white glossy decorating gel
black glossy decorating gel

WITCH

1 black and orange licorice allsort
2 orange mini M&M's
1 orange Crazy Banana
green colouring
black glossy decorating gel

1 Preheat oven to moderate; line six holes of 12-hole (⅓ cup/80ml) muffin pan with patty cases. Make cake according to directions on packet, pour ¼ cup mixture into each hole; bake in moderate oven about 20 minutes. Stand cakes in pan 5 minutes; turn onto wire rack to cool.

2 SNAKES Cut 1.5cm deep hollow from centre of one patty cake. Tint ⅙ of the butter cream with green colouring; spread over hollowed cake. Position ends of Brite Crawlers in hollow. Using black decorating gel, dot eyes on snakes.

3 EYEBALL Tint ⅙ of the butter cream with red colouring; spread over one patty cake. Trim tip of large marshmallow; centre in cake for white of eye. Position giant Smartie on marshmallow for pupil. Using white decorating gel, pipe veins around white of eye on red butter cream.

4 BAT Tint ⅙ of the butter cream with red colouring; spread over one patty cake. Centre jelly bean for bat's body. Cut two wings from licorice strap; position on either side of body. Using white decorating gel, pipe clouds on red butter cream for sky and eyes on bat; using black decorating gel, dot pupils on eyes. Position stars on red butter cream.

5 GHOSTS Tint ⅙ of the butter cream with black colouring; spread over one patty cake. Cut milk bottles into ghost shapes; position on cake. Using black decorating gel, dot eyes on ghosts.

6 CAT Tint ⅙ of the butter cream with blue colouring; spread over one patty cake. Position giant Smartie on cake for body and Smartie for head. Cut small piece of licorice strap into thin strip; position on body for tail. Cut small piece of licorice strap into two small triangles; position on head for ears. Position Crazy Banana on blue butter cream for moon; position stars on blue butter cream. Using white decorating gel, pipe eyes on cat; using black decorating gel, dot pupils on eyes.

7 WITCH Reserve 1 tablespoon of remaining ⅙ of the butter cream in small bowl. Tint remaining butter cream with red colouring; spread over remaining patty cake. Slice a thin strip off allsort, trim into triangle; position for witch's hat. Using remainder of allsort, cut black pieces into two thin strips; position on cake for hat brim. Position M&M's for eyes; position Crazy Banana for nose. Tint reserved butter cream with green colouring. Spoon into piping bag (page 115); pipe hair onto witch. Using black decorating gel, dot pupils, nose bump and mouth on witch.

tips The cake mix is enough to make 12 patty cakes, so decorate the other six patty cakes with your own little cakes of horror.

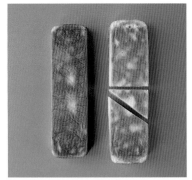

Leave one bar cake whole. Cut the other bar cake into three pieces, as shown

Assemble the cake pieces on the board to form the number; discard remaining cake

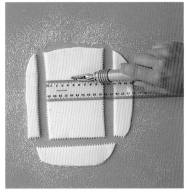

Using a pastry wheel and ruler as a guide, cut a 10cm square from yellow icing for quilt

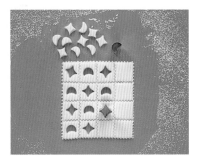

Use tiny cutters or a small sharp-pointed knife to cut moon and star shapes from the quilt

one

cake

340g packet buttercake mix
23cm x 51cm prepared board (page 112)
1 quantity butter cream (page 112)
blue colouring

decorations

icing sugar mixture
250g ready-made soft icing
yellow, green and pink colouring
22 coloured cachous
small teddy bear or doll

1 Preheat oven to moderate; grease and line (page 110) two 8cm x 25cm bar cake pans. Make cake according to directions on packet, divide mixture between pans; bake in moderate oven about 25 minutes. Stand cakes in pans 5 minutes; turn onto wire rack to cool. Using serrated knife, level cake tops so cakes are the same height.

2 Cut one cake into three pieces, as shown. Assemble cake pieces on board, cut-side down, to form number; discard remaining cake.

3 Tint butter cream with blue colouring; spread all over cake.

4 On surface dusted with icing sugar, knead icing until smooth. Roll ½ of the icing until 3mm thick, cut 11cm square for sheet; cover sheet and enclose white trimmings in plastic wrap.

5 Knead yellow colouring into remaining icing; roll until 3mm thick. Using pastry wheel and ruler, cut 10cm square for quilt; enclose yellow trimmings in plastic wrap. Using ruler, mark 2.5cm intervals on all four quilt edges. Using pastry wheel, ruler and markings as guides, gently roll wheel across icing to make quilt pattern.

6 Using tiny cutters or sharp-pointed knife, cut moon and star shapes from quilt; cover quilt with plastic wrap. Position shapes at top of cake with 10 of the cachous; shape yellow trimmings into pillow, place on cake. Position sheet on cake, top with quilt; turn down edge.

7 Divide reserved white trimmings in half. Knead green colouring into one half of the white trimmings and pink into the other half; roll each until 3mm thick. Using tiny cutters or sharp-pointed knife, cut heart shapes; position with remaining cachous on cake. Position bear or doll near pillow.

tips One-year-olds may be too young to eat the cachous, but they'll certainly love the cake.
Tiny heart-, star-, moon- and other-shaped cutters are sometimes sold as aspic cutters.

two

You need approximately two boxes of Runts.

cake

2 x 340g packets buttercake mix
33cm x 41cm prepared board (page 112)
2 quantities butter cream (page 112)
blue and yellow colouring

decorations

1 yellow jube
10 banana Runts
1 green Fruit Stick
1 spearmint leaf
2 yellow Mini Fruits
6 red Mini Fruits
6 orange Mini Fruits
2 chocolate bees

Place square cake on the board; place bar cake at the bottom edge of the square cake

Using a small serrated knife, cut around the paper pattern to form the number

1 Preheat oven to moderate; grease and line (page 110) deep 23cm-square cake pan and 8cm x 25cm bar cake pan. Make cake according to directions on packet, pour ⅔ of the mixture into square pan and remaining mixture into bar cake pan; bake square cake in moderate oven about 40 minutes and bar cake about 25 minutes. Stand cakes in pans 5 minutes; turn onto wire rack to cool. Using serrated knife, level cake tops so cakes are the same height.

2 Place square cake on board, cut-side down. Place bar cake at bottom edge of square cake, cut-side down. Using paper pattern (page 112) from pattern sheet, cut out number.

3 Tint ¾ of the butter cream with blue colouring; spread all over cake.

4 Swirl yellow colouring into remaining butter cream for marbled effect. Spoon butter cream into piping bag (page 115) fitted with 1cm plain tube; pipe beehive on cake.

5 Make sun from yellow jube and banana Runts. Cut Fruit Stick in half, slice thinly lengthways; position on cake for flower stems. Cut spearmint leaf in half through centre; position on stems. Make flowers from coloured Mini Fruits; position chocolate bees on cake.

three

cake

2 x 340g packets buttercake mix
30cm x 43cm prepared board (page 112)
1½ quantities butter cream (page 112)
blue colouring

decorations

icing sugar mixture
250g ready-made soft icing
green colouring
1 artificial water lily
3 chocolate frogs

1 Preheat oven to moderate; grease and line (page 110) two 20cm ring pans. Make cake according to directions on packet, divide mixture between pans; bake in moderate oven about 35 minutes. Stand cakes in pans 5 minutes; turn onto wire rack to cool. Using serrated knife, level cake tops so cakes are the same height.

2 Place cakes cut-side down. Cut segments from cakes, as shown.

3 Assemble cake pieces on board, cut-side down, to form number; discard remaining cake.

4 Tint butter cream with blue colouring; spread all over cake.

5 On surface dusted with icing sugar, knead icing until smooth. Knead green colouring into icing; roll until 3mm thick.

6 Using paper pattern (page 112) from pattern sheet and a sharp-pointed knife, cut five lily leaves from icing. Using same knife, gently mark veins on leaves; drape over rolling pin to dry. Position leaves on cake with water lily and chocolate frogs.

tips Transpose the leaf pattern onto cardboard, then use the cardboard leaf as a guide when cutting the leaf shapes from icing.
The leaves can be made up to 3 days ahead; store in an airtight container.

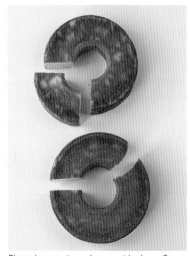

Place the two ring cakes cut-side down. Cut segments out of the ring cakes, as shown

Assemble the cake pieces on board to form the number; discard remaining cake pieces

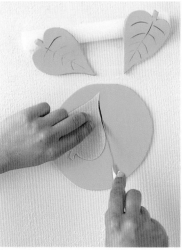

Using the leaf pattern, cut five lily leaves from the icing then drape over a rolling pin to dry

Place cake cut-side down. Using a serrated knife, cut the cake into three even strips

Leave the centre strip whole; cut the two remaining strips into segments, as shown

Assemble cake pieces on the board to form the number; discard remaining cake pieces

four

cake

2 x 340g packets buttercake mix
40cm-square prepared board (page 112)
1½ quantities butter cream (page 112)
red colouring

decorations

icing sugar mixture
250g ready-made soft icing
black colouring
19 Tic Tac mints
1 black licorice strap
4 chocolate cars
assorted mini road signs

1 Preheat oven to moderate; grease and line (page 110) 20cm x 30cm lamington pan. Make cake according to directions on packet, pour enough mixture into pan to come almost level to the top; bake in moderate oven about 35 minutes. Stand cake in pan 5 minutes; turn onto wire rack to cool. Using serrated knife, level cake top.

2 Place cake cut-side down. Cut cake into three even strips.

3 Leave centre strip whole; cut remaining strips into three segments, as shown.

4 Assemble cake pieces on board, cut-side down, to form number; discard remaining cake.

5 Tint butter cream with red colouring; spread all over cake.

6 On surface dusted with icing sugar, knead icing until smooth; reserve a walnut-sized amount of icing for road markings, enclose in plastic wrap.

7 Knead black colouring into icing to make grey colour; roll until 2mm thick. Using sharp knife, cut 6.5cm x 28cm rectangle, 6.5cm x 15cm rectangle and 6.5cm x 8cm rectangle; position on cake for roads.

8 Roll reserved white icing into thin cord, cut into two 6.5cm pieces and one 27cm piece; secure to cake, with tiny dabs of water, for road markings.

9 Secure Tic Tac mints to roads, with tiny dabs of water, to mark lanes. Cut licorice strap into fourteen 1cm pieces and one 13cm piece; position on cake to form rail tracks. Position cars and road signs on cake, as desired; secure with a little butter cream.

tip Make patty cakes from any leftover cake mixture.

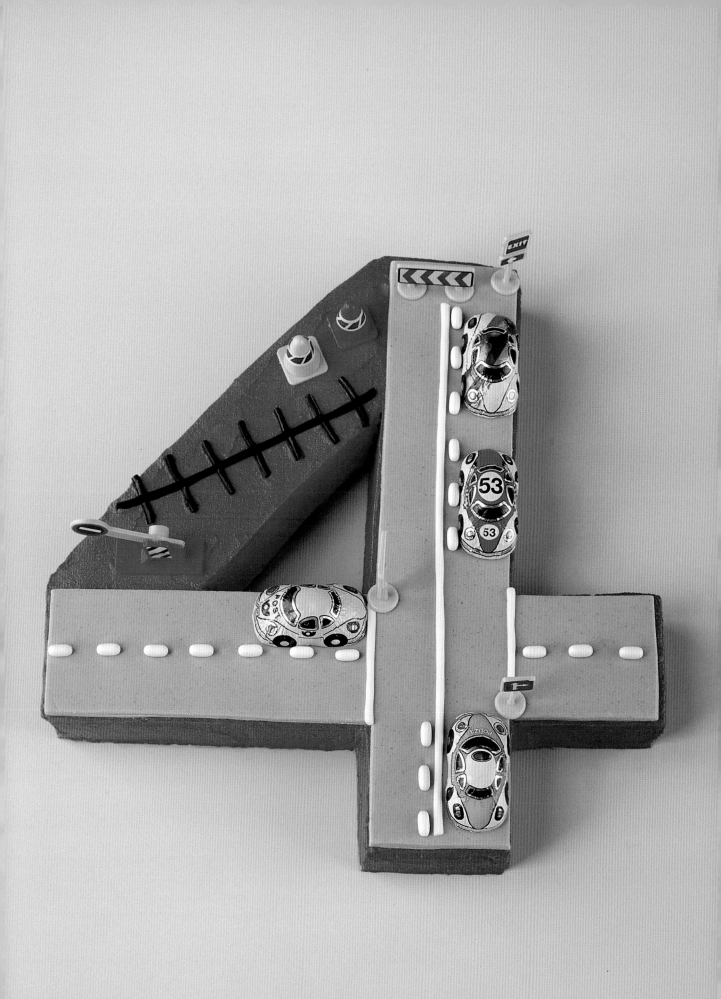

Using a piping bag fitted with a 1cm plain tube, pipe five grubs onto an oven tray

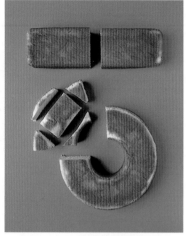

Cut the bar cake in half widthways, cut the ring cake into small segments, as shown

Assemble the cake pieces on the board to form the number; discard remaining cake pieces

five

meringue grubs

1 egg white
¾ cup (165g) caster sugar
¼ teaspoon cream of tartar
2 tablespoons boiling water
coloured sprinkles
10 coloured cachous

cake

340g packet buttercake mix
30cm x 45cm prepared board (page 112)
1½ quantities butter cream (page 112)
pink food colouring

decorations

36 mini pink musk sticks
36 love heart Runts
1 green Fruit Stick
11 spearmint leaves

1 Preheat oven to very slow. Combine egg white, sugar, cream of tartar and the water in small bowl. Bring small saucepan of water to a boil; reduce heat to a simmer. Place bowl over saucepan, taking care that water level does not touch bottom of bowl. Beat egg white mixture with electric mixer about 7 minutes or until sugar is dissolved and stiff peaks form. Remove bowl from heat; spoon egg white mixture immediately into large piping bag (page 115) fitted with 1cm plain tube. Pipe five grubs onto oven tray lined with baking paper. Top grubs with coloured sprinkles; position cachous on grubs for eyes. Bake in very slow oven about 30 minutes or until grubs are dry to touch; cool. Grubs can be made up to a week ahead; store in an airtight container.

2 Preheat oven to moderate; grease and line (page 110) 8cm x 25cm bar cake pan and 20cm ring pan. Make cake according to directions on packet, divide mixture between pans so both mixtures are to the same depth; bake in moderate oven about 25 minutes. Stand cakes in pans 5 minutes; turn onto wire rack to cool. Using serrated knife, level cake tops so cakes are the same height.

3 Place cakes cut-side down. Cut bar cake in half widthways; cut ring cake into segments, as shown.

4 Assemble cake pieces on board, cut-side down, to form number; discard remaining cake.

5 Tint butter cream with pink colouring; spread all over cake.

6 Position meringue grubs on cake; decorate sides of cake with musk sticks and Runts. Thinly slice Fruit Stick lengthways; position on cake for stems. Split spearmint leaves in half through centre for leaves; cut a few "nibbles" out of a leaf or two. Position leaves on cake.

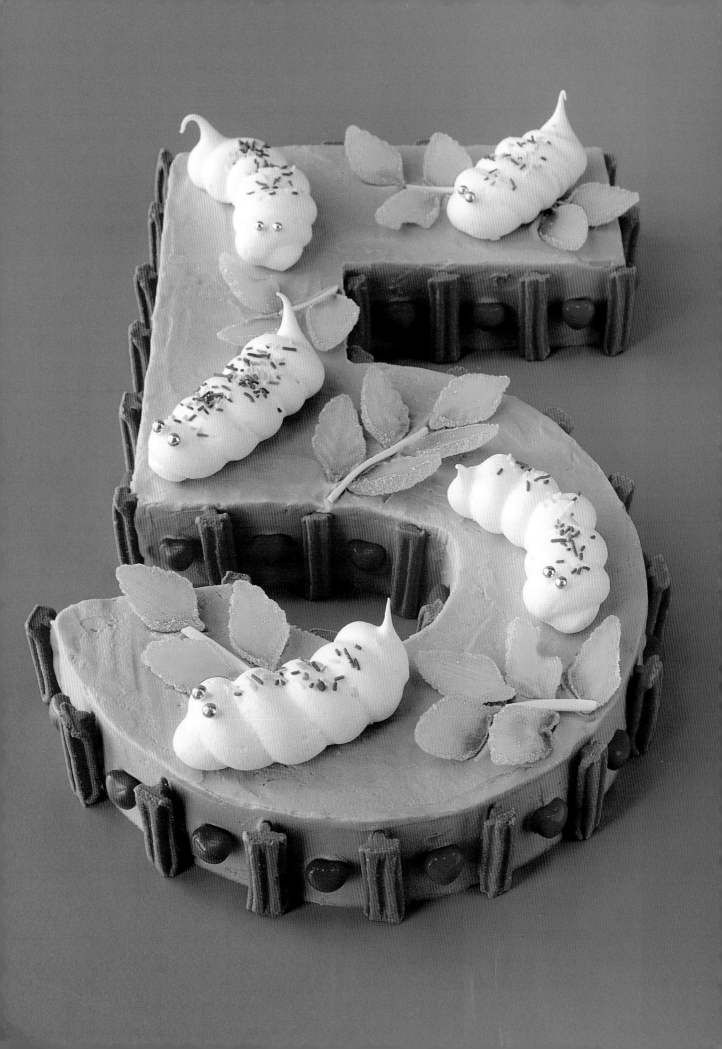

six

cake

340g packet buttercake mix
30cm x 44cm prepared board (page 112)
1½ quantities butter cream (page 112)
black and red colouring

decorations

2 bananas
8cm green Bubble Tape (bubble gum)
1 black licorice strap
2 green M&M's
1 milk bottle, halved lengthways

1 Preheat oven to moderate; grease and line (page 110) 8cm x 25cm bar cake pan and 20cm ring pan. Make cake according to directions on packet, divide mixture between pans so both mixtures are to the same depth; bake in moderate oven about 25 minutes. Stand cakes in pans 5 minutes; turn onto wire rack to cool. Using serrated knife, level cake tops so cakes are the same height.

2 Using paper pattern (page 112) from pattern sheet, cut tail from bar cake, cut-side down.

3 Assemble cake pieces on board, cut-side down, to form number; discard remaining cake.

4 Tint ¼ of the butter cream with black colouring; spread over widow's peak and end of tail. Tint remaining butter cream with red colouring; spread over remaining cake.

5 Trim banana ends diagonally; position on cake for horns. Cut eyes from Bubble Tape; position on cake. Cut 8cm piece from licorice strap; outline eyes. Position M&M's on cake for eye irises.

6 Cut eyebrows, mouth and goatee from remaining licorice; position on cake. Trim milk bottle halves for fangs; position on cake.

Leave the ring cake whole, lay the paper pattern on the bar cake for devil's tail

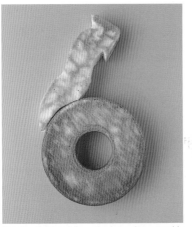

Cut the devil's tail from the bar cake; assemble cake pieces on board to form the number

Leave one bar cake whole, cut the other bar cake into two pieces, as shown

Assemble the cake pieces on the board, cut-side down, to form the number

Twist four chenille sticks together at the centre; bend the ends to make spider legs

seven

choc-crackle spiders

1 cup (35g) rice bubbles
1 cup (70g) shredded coconut
1 tablespoon cocoa powder
1 tablespoon icing sugar mixture
100g dark chocolate, melted
30g butter, melted

cake

340g packet buttercake mix
31cm x 47cm prepared board (page 112)
1 quantity butter cream (page 112)
orange and black colouring

decorations

28 x 15cm (3mm) black chenille sticks (pipe cleaners)
14 Skittles

1 Combine rice bubbles, coconut, sifted cocoa and icing sugar in medium bowl. Using fork, mix in chocolate and butter. Spoon level tablespoons of mixture into two 12-hole mini (1 tablespoon/20ml) muffin tins. Refrigerate about 1 hour or until spider bodies set.

2 Preheat oven to moderate; grease and line (page 110) two 8cm x 25cm bar cake pans. Make cake according to directions on packet, divide cake mixture between pans; bake in moderate oven about 25 minutes. Stand cakes in pans 5 minutes; turn onto wire rack to cool. Using serrated knife, level cake tops so cakes are the same height.

3 Cut one cake into two pieces, as shown.

4 Assemble cake pieces on board, cut-side down, to form number.

5 Tint ¾ of the butter cream with orange colouring; spread all over cake. Tint remaining butter cream with black colouring; spoon into piping bag (page 115) fitted with 2mm plain tube, pipe spider webs onto cake and board.

6 Twist four chenille sticks together at centre; bend ends to make spider legs. Position legs on cake; top with one spider body. Using leftover icing, attach Skittles onto spiders for eyes; pipe a little black icing on Skittles for eye pupils. Repeat with remaining chenille sticks, spider bodies, black butter cream and Skittles.

tips This recipe makes 24 choc-crackle spiders; serve the extras as an accompaniment or, if you have extra chenille sticks and Skittles, make more spiders to decorate the cake board or give one spider to each guest. Chocolate and butter can be melted together over hot water or in a microwave oven on HIGH (100%) for about 1 minute.

eight

cake

2 x 340g packets buttercake mix
30cm x 48cm prepared board (page 112)
2 quantities butter cream (page 112)
yellow colouring

decorations

40 boiled lollies
8 giant black Smarties

1 Preheat oven to moderate; grease and line (page 110) two 20cm ring pans. Make cake according to directions on packet, divide mixture between pans; bake in moderate oven about 35 minutes. Stand cakes in pans 5 minutes; turn onto wire rack to cool. Using serrated knife, level cake tops so cakes are the same height.
2 Trim a shallow arc from one cake, as shown.
3 Assemble cake pieces on board, cut-side down, to form number; discard remaining cake.
4 Tint butter cream with yellow colouring; spread over top and sides of cake.
5 Arrange boiled lollies and Smarties on cake for flowers.

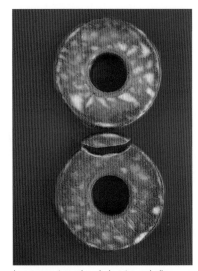

Leave one ring cake whole; trim a shallow arc from the edge of the other ring cake

Assemble the cake pieces on the board to form the number; discard remaining cake

nine

cake

340g packet buttercake mix
30cm x 49cm prepared board (page 112)
1½ quantities butter cream (page 112)
green colouring

decorations

9 chocolate ladybirds
9 spearmint leaves

1 Preheat oven to moderate; grease and line (page 110) 8cm x 25cm bar
   cake pan and 20cm ring pan. Make cake according to directions on packet,
   divide cake mixture between pans so both mixtures are to the same depth;
   bake in moderate oven about 25 minutes. Stand cakes in pans 5 minutes;
   turn onto wire rack to cool. Using serrated knife, level cake tops so cakes
   are the same height.

2 Cut bar cake into three segments, as shown.

3 Assemble cake pieces on board, cut-side down, to form number; discard
   remaining cake.

4 Tint butter cream with green colouring; spread ¾ of the butter cream over cake.

5 Tint remaining butter cream with more colouring to make a deeper green;
   spoon into piping bag (page 115) fitted with 4mm plain tube, pipe vine and
   tendrils onto cake. Position chocolate ladybirds and spearmint leaves on cake.

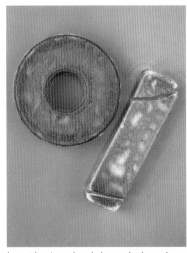

*Leave the ring cake whole; cut the bar cake
into three segments, cut-side down*

*Assemble the cake pieces on the board to
form the number; discard remaining cake*

basic know-how

We used packet cake mixes throughout this book to ensure consistency of size and texture. However, if you would prefer to make your own cake, we have included four fabulously easy and delicious recipes in these information pages to use as your starting point.

NB *The patterns supplied for cakes on the pattern sheet (see centre of book) are of actual size.*

Making the cake

For best results:

● Use an electric mixer when beating the cake mixture
● Follow the directions on the packet
● Have all ingredients at room temperature
● A large mixing bowl should have the capacity to hold 4 packet mixes. It's best to mix single packets in a small bowl, and 2 or 3 packets in a medium bowl

Baking cakes together

You can bake cakes together, either on the same oven shelf or on different shelves. The important thing is that the cake pans do not touch each other, the sides of the oven or the door. If baking cakes on the same shelf, exchange the positions of the pans about halfway through baking time.

If baking cakes on different shelves, make certain there is enough room for the cake on the lower shelf to rise without touching the bottom of the shelf above it. Change the cakes from the lower to the upper shelf positions about halfway through baking time for even browning.

When small cakes are baked with larger cakes (which have longer baking times), place the small ones toward the front of the oven then, when the small cakes are baked, move the large cakes into that position to complete their baking time.

When two or more cakes are being baked in the oven at the same time, the baking time may be slightly longer than specified in recipes. A perfectly baked cake should feel firm to the touch and be slightly shrunken from the side(s) of the pan. There should not be any need to test with a skewer. However, if in doubt, test by inserting a metal skewer into the centre of the cake; if any mixture clings to the skewer, the cake needs a little more baking time. Never test a sponge cake with a skewer; instead, gently press the surface of cake with fingertips – it should feel firm.

Cake pans

Each recipe specifies the required pan size(s) and exact quantities required to make your cakes look the same as ours. However, cake sizes and shapes can be changed to suit yourself and your chosen decorations.

Use rigid, straight-sided, deep cake pans. The ones we used are made from good quality tin or aluminium.

Greasing and lining the cake pan

All cake pans were greased lightly but evenly with a pastry brush dipped in a little melted butter. An alternative method is to spray pans with cooking-oil spray. We lined the bases of the pans with baking paper. To fit baking paper, place your pan, right-side up, on a piece of baking paper, then trace around the pan's base with a pencil. Cut the paper shape just slightly inside the marked area, to allow for the thickness of the pan. We also lined the side(s) of the cake pans so the paper extended above the pan.

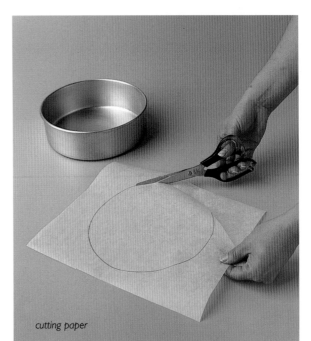

cutting paper

lining base and side of tin

Cake recipes

Each of these recipes makes a cake equal in quantity to one 340g packet of White Wings Golden Buttercake Cake Mix. Therefore, if the particular recipe you've decided to make calls for 2 packets of cake mix, double the quantities called for and adjust the baking time. These four cake recipes will bake in approximately the same time as the packet mixes.

Basic butter cake
125g butter, softened
1 teaspoon vanilla essence
¾ cup (165g) caster sugar
2 eggs
1½ cups (225g) self-raising flour
½ cup (125ml) milk

Preheat oven to moderate. Grease (and line) pan(s).

Beat butter, essence and sugar in small bowl with electric mixer until light and fluffy. Beat in eggs, one at a time, until combined. Stir in flour and milk, in two batches. Spread mixture into prepared pan(s). Bake in moderate oven until cake is cooked. Stand cake in pan(s) about 5 minutes; turn onto wire rack to cool.

To marble a butter cake, place portions of cake mixture in different bowls then tint each with desired colour. Dollop spoonfuls of mixture into prepared pan(s), alternating colours, then gently swirl together with a skewer or spoon, to create marbled effect.

Rich chocolate cake
1⅓ cups (200g) self-raising flour
½ cup (50g) cocoa powder
125g butter, softened
1 teaspoon vanilla essence
1¼ cups (275g) caster sugar
2 eggs
⅔ cup (160ml) water

Preheat oven to moderate. Grease (and line) pan(s).

Sift flour and cocoa into medium bowl, add remaining ingredients; beat on low speed with electric mixer until ingredients are combined. Increase speed to medium; beat about 3 minutes or until mixture is smooth and changed to a lighter colour. Spread into prepared pan(s). Bake in moderate oven until cake is cooked. Stand cake in pan(s) about 5 minutes; turn onto wire rack to cool.

Best-ever sponge

The only liquid called for in this recipe comes from the eggs; for best results, they should be at room temperature.

3 eggs
½ cup (110g) caster sugar
¼ cup (35g) cornflour
¼ cup (35g) plain flour
¼ cup (35g) self-raising flour

Preheat oven to moderate. Grease (and line) pan(s).

Beat eggs in small bowl with electric mixer until thick and creamy (this will take about 8 minutes). Add sugar, 1 tablespoon at a time, beating after each addition, until sugar dissolves; transfer mixture to large bowl. Sift dry ingredients together three times then sift evenly over egg mixture; fold in gently. Spread into prepared pan(s). Bake in moderate oven until cake is cooked. Turn immediately onto wire rack to cool.

Wheat-free sponge

This is a gluten-free cake, perfect for people who suffer from coeliac disease and do not tolerate wheat flour. Cornflour, also called cornstarch in some countries, is made from corn kernels and contains no gluten. Use care when purchasing cornflour because there is a wheaten cornflour available which, as the name suggests, contains wheat.

3 eggs
½ cup (110g) caster sugar
¾ cup (110g) cornflour (100% corn)

Preheat oven to moderate. Grease (and line) pan(s).

Beat eggs in small bowl with electric mixer until thick and creamy (this will take about 8 minutes). Add sugar, 1 tablespoon at a time, beating after each addition until sugar dissolves. Sift cornflour three times then sift evenly over egg mixture; fold in gently. Spread into prepared pan(s). Bake in moderate oven until cake is cooked. Turn immediately onto wire rack to cool.

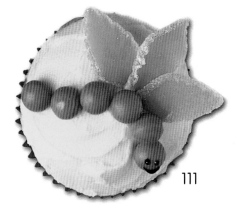

111

Preparing the cake(s)

Trim cooked cake(s) so it sits flat or joins neatly to another cake.

trimming cake with serrated knife

Most cakes in this book use the smooth base as the top of the finished cake; in this case, it's a good idea to cool the cake upside down. Some cakes are decorated top-side up.

Crumbs can present problems when they become mixed with the icing. To prevent this from happening, bake cake the day before you decorate it. After the cake cools, keep it in an airtight container in the refrigerator overnight. Decorate cake while it is still cold. If you think you will take longer than 30 minutes to decorate your cake, freeze it, uncovered, for 30 minutes, before decorating.

Cake boards

Some of the cakes in this book call for a cake board which becomes part of the decoration. In any case, the board makes the cake easy to handle as well as more attractive.

Place cake(s), as directed, on a board that has been covered with greaseproof decorative paper, contact, or any type of patterned foil-like gift wrapping. We've given an approximate cake-board size in almost all of the recipes, allowing some space around the cake. Using masonite or a similarly strong board, cut your selected paper 5cm to 10cm larger than the shape of the board. A variety of sizes of boards can be bought, already covered in paper, from cake-decorating suppliers and some craft shops.

Using paper patterns

If you choose to make a cake that is based on a pattern, you will find the template on the pattern sheet in the middle of this book. Using a pencil, trace the pattern onto baking or greaseproof paper. Carefully cut around this paper tracing. Assemble cake pieces as directed in the recipe method, then place the paper pattern on top of cake. Using toothpicks, secure pattern onto cake. Using a small serrated knife, cut around the pattern to form the shape of the cake. Remove toothpicks and pattern, then proceed with recipe.

If you are cutting shapes from ready-made soft icing using a paper pattern, use the above method but do not use toothpicks to secure the pattern to icing. Use a small sharp-pointed knife to cut around the pattern.

If you are cutting shapes from fabric using a paper pattern, use the original method to create the pattern, then use pins to attach the pattern to fabric and scissors to cut around pattern.

Choosing the covering

We used either ready-made soft icing, butter cream or fluffy frosting, depending on the effect we desired. Ready-made soft icing is easy to use and gives a smooth surface to the cake. Butter cream is a little harder to spread than fluffy frosting, but you can work with butter cream longer than with fluffy frosting, which tends to set. Fluffy frosting is good for fluffy or snowy effects, but it is fairly difficult to make smooth.

The yellow colour of the butter cream will affect the colour you choose. For example, if you add rose pink, the cream tends to become salmon pink; if you add red, it becomes apricot and so on. If you use ready-made soft icing or fluffy frosting, you have a white base to colour from.

Use a spatula or palette knife for spreading and swirling butter cream or fluffy frosting.

Butter cream

This is a basic butter cream (also known as vienna cream) recipe; the flavour can be varied by adding finely grated rind of any citrus fruit, etc, or any essence to your taste.

125g butter, softened
1½ cups (240g) icing sugar mixture
2 tablespoons milk

Beat butter in small bowl with electric mixer until as white as possible. Gradually beat in half of the icing sugar, milk, then remaining icing sugar. Flavour and colour as required.

Chocolate variation: Sift ⅓ cup (35g) cocoa powder in with the first batch of icing sugar.

Ready-made soft icing

Ready-made soft icing can be bought from cake-decorating suppliers and some health food shops, delicatessens and supermarkets. There are several brands available, and they can be sold as Soft Icing, Prepared Icing or Ready to Roll Icing. All are easy to handle; knead the icing gently on a surface dusted with icing sugar mixture until it is smooth.

Brush warmed strained apricot jam lightly and evenly all over cake. Roll icing until it is about 7mm thick. Lift icing onto cake with rolling pin. Smooth the icing with hands dusted with icing sugar, easing it around the side(s) and base of cake. Push icing in around the base of cake then cut away any excess with a sharp knife.

covering square board

covering round board

kneading colouring into ready-made soft icing

colouring butter cream

Fluffy frosting

1 cup (220g) caster sugar
⅓ cup (80ml) water
2 egg whites

Combine sugar and the water in small saucepan; stir
with a wooden spoon over high heat, without boiling,
until sugar dissolves. Boil, uncovered, without stirring,
about 3 to 5 minutes or until syrup is slightly thick.
If a candy thermometer is available, the syrup will be
ready when it reaches 114°C (240°F).

Otherwise, when the syrup is thick, remove the pan
from the heat, allow the bubbles to subside then test the
syrup by dropping 1 teaspoon into a cup of cold water.
The syrup should form a ball of soft sticky toffee when
rolled gently between your fingertips.

The syrup should not change colour; if it does, it has
been cooked for too long and you will have to discard it
and start again.

While syrup is boiling, beat egg whites in small bowl
with electric mixer until stiff; keep beating (or whites will
deflate) until syrup reaches the correct temperature.

When syrup is ready, allow bubbles to subside then
pour a very thin stream onto the egg whites with mixer
operating on medium speed. If syrup is added too quickly
to the egg whites, frosting will not thicken. Continue
beating and adding syrup until all syrup is used.
Continue to beat until frosting stands in stiff peaks
(frosting should be barely warm by this stage).

Tint frosting, if desired, by beating food colouring
through while mixing, or by stirring through with spatula
at the end. Frosting can also be flavoured with a little
of any essence of your choice.

For best results, frosting should be applied to a cake
on the day it is to be served, while the frosting is still
soft and has a marshmallow consistency. While you can
frost the cake the day before, the frosting will become crisp
and lose its glossy appearance, much like a meringue.

Make sure to frost the cake around the base near the
board; this forms a seal and helps keep the cake fresh.

Piping gel

Piping gel is sold in small tubes at supermarkets.
If you prefer, make your own using the recipe below.
Store the mixture in an airtight container in the
refrigerator for up to a month; if it becomes too thick,
stir in a tiny amount of water, a little at a time, until
gel reaches a pipable consistency.

⅓ cup (75g) caster sugar
1 tablespoon cornflour
¼ cup (60ml) lemon juice
¼ cup (60ml) water

Combine sugar and cornflour in small saucepan;
gradually blend in juice then the water. Stir over
high heat until mixture boils and thickens.
Colour as desired.

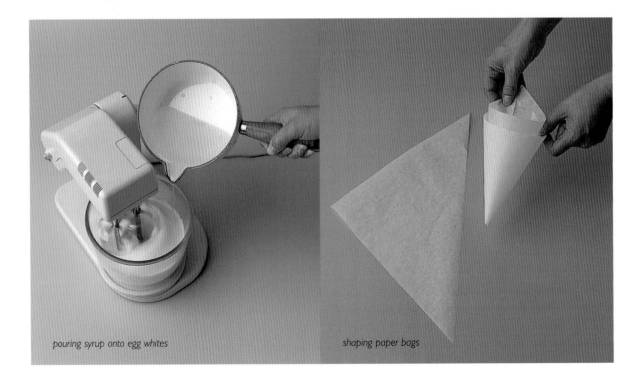

pouring syrup onto egg whites   *shaping paper bags*

Equipment

Piping bags can be bought from cake-decorating or chefs' suppliers; these are usually made from a waterproof fabric, and can have screws attached to hold icing tubes.

Alternatively, you can make bags from baking or greaseproof paper, which will hold various-shaped tubes. You can also cut the tips of the bags to the size you require. These are ideal for small amounts of icing or chocolate.

Another option is to use a small plastic bag. Push the icing (or chocolate) into the corner of the bag, twist the bag around the icing, then snip the tip to the desired size and shape.

Icing tubes are made from metal or plastic, and can be bought from cake-decorating suppliers, some craft shops, supermarkets and cookware shops.

Non-stick rolling pins are available from cake-decorating and chefs' suppliers as well as cookware shops.

Candy thermometers, used to measure the temperature of syrup, are available from hardware and cookware shops.

We used double-ended toothpicks throughout this book.

Candy cake decorations, made from sugar, corn starch and vegetable gum, are assorted lettering, pictures and shapes used for decorating cakes. These can easily be found at your local supermarket.

Food colourings

We used good-quality edible gels and concentrated pastes, which are available from cake-decorating suppliers and some health food stores. It's best to add minuscule amounts (using a skewer or toothpick) to the icing until the desired colour is reached. Use care when handling food colourings as they stain. Coloured icing can become darker or lighter on standing, so keep this in mind when decorating a cake ahead of time. If you have the time, it's a good idea to experiment by colouring a small amount of the icing, then covering it with plastic wrap and allowing it to stand for a few hours to determine if the icing fades or darkens.

various items of cake decorating equipment

piping bags and icing tubes

decorations

cachous

Fruit Sticks

Chunky Raspberry Twister

musk stick

mini musk stick

Super Rope licorice

M&M's

mini M&M's

jubes

raspberry

Mini Fruits

spearmint leaves

Skittles

Crazy Bananas

banana

Runts

Twinkle Sprinkles

chocolate freckle

coloured sprinkles

Tic Tac mints

Sour Ball

milk bottle

cake decorating hearts

cake decorating moon

cake decorating stars

Jelly Tot

large teeth lolly

strawberries & cream

giant Smarties

Wonka

Oompa

Jaffa

Smarties

boiled lollies

giant Jaffa

pineapple

gummy feet

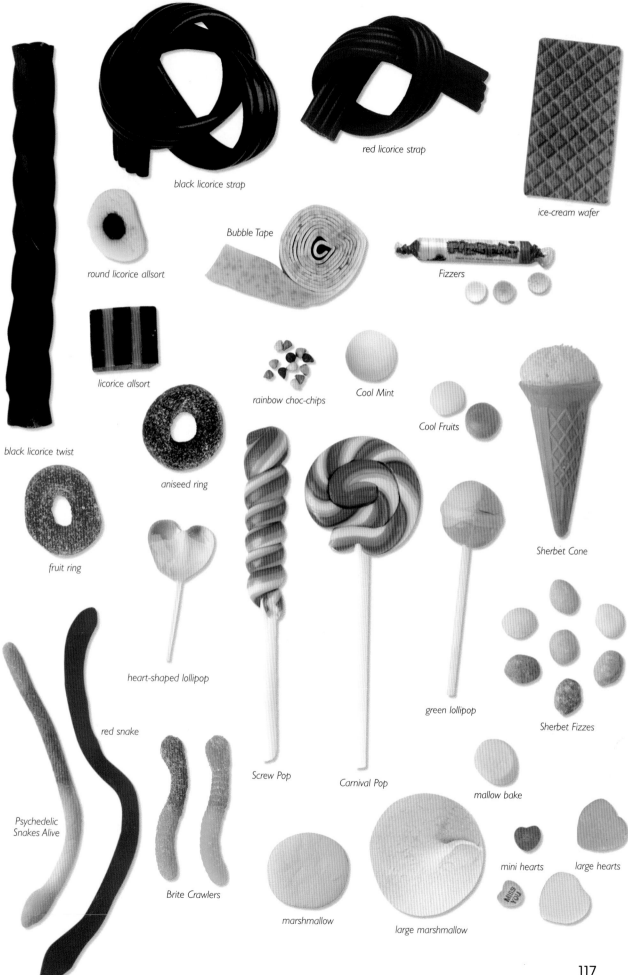

black licorice strap

red licorice strap

ice-cream wafer

round licorice allsort

Bubble Tape

Fizzers

licorice allsort

rainbow choc-chips

Cool Mint

Cool Fruits

black licorice twist

aniseed ring

Sherbet Cone

fruit ring

heart-shaped lollipop

green lollipop

Sherbet Fizzes

red snake

Screw Pop

Carnival Pop

mallow bake

Psychedelic
Snakes Alive

mini hearts

large hearts

Brite Crawlers

marshmallow

large marshmallow

MISS YOU!

Flake

Curly Wurly

white chocolate Melts

milk chocolate Melts

Toblerone piece

milk chocolate block

mint stick

gold-covered sugared almond

silver-covered sugared almond

green frog

Life Saver

red frog

Five Flavours Life Savers

jelly beans

large chocolate gold coin

Bo-Peep

small chocolate gold coin

medium chocolate gold coin

glossary

butter use salted or unsalted (sweet) butter; 125g is equal to 1 stick butter.

cocoa powder also just called cocoa; unsweetened, dried, roasted then ground cocoa beans.

coconut, shredded thin strips of dried coconut.

cornflour also known as cornstarch; a thickening agent in cooking.

cream of tartar the acid ingredient in baking powder; added to confectionery mixtures to help prevent sugar crystallising. Keeps frostings creamy and improves volume when beating egg whites.

dark chocolate we used premium-quality dark eating chocolate rather than compound.

dolly varden pan spherical, bombe-shaped cake pan.

flour
    plain an all-purpose flour, made from wheat.
    self-raising plain flour sifted with baking powder in the proportion of 1 cup flour to 2 teaspoons baking powder.

ice magic a chocolate coating for ice-cream; sets quickly.

ice-cream use good quality ice-cream; actual ice-cream varieties differ from manufacturer to manufacturer depending on the quantities of air and fat that are incorporated into the mixture.

lamington pan 20cm x 30cm slab cake pan, 3cm deep.

lollies also known as sweets.

milk we used full-cream homogenised milk unless otherwise specified.

rice bubbles also known as Rice Crispies; puffed rice product made with malt extract (which contains gluten).

sugar
    caster also known as superfine or finely granulated table sugar.
    mixture, icing also known as confectioners' sugar or powdered sugar; granulated sugar crushed together with a small amount (about 3%) of cornflour.
    pure icing also known as confectioners' sugar or powdered sugar.
    white we used coarse, granulated table sugar, unless otherwise specified.

vanilla essence an inexpensive substitute for pure vanilla extract, made with synthetic vanillin and other flavourings.

vegetable oil any of a number of oils sourced from plants rather than animal fats.

facts and figures

Wherever you live, you'll be able to use our recipes with the help of these easy-to-follow conversions. While these conversions are approximate only, the difference between an exact and the approximate conversion of various liquid and dry measures is minimal and will not affect your cooking results.

oven temperatures

These oven temperatures are only a guide. Always check the manufacturer's manual.

	°C (Celsius)	°F (Fahrenheit)	Gas mark
Very slow	120	250	½
Slow	140-150	275-300	1-2
Moderately slow	170	325	3
Moderate	180-190	350-375	4-5
Moderately hot	200	400	6
Hot	220-230	425-450	7-8
Very hot	240	475	9

measuring equipment

The difference between one country's measuring cups and another's is, at most, within a 2 or 3 teaspoon variance. (For the record, 1 Australian metric measuring cup holds approximately 250ml.) The most accurate way of measuring dry ingredients is to weigh them. When measuring liquids, use a clear glass or plastic jug with the metric markings. (One Australian metric tablespoon holds 20ml; one Australian metric teaspoon holds 5ml.)

If you would like to purchase *The Australian Women's Weekly* Test Kitchen's metric measuring cups and spoons (as approved by Standards Australia), turn to page 120 for details and order coupon. You will receive:

- a graduated set of four cups for measuring dry ingredients, with sizes marked on the cups.
- a graduated set of four spoons for measuring dry and liquid ingredients, with amounts marked on the spoons.

Note: North America, NZ and the UK use 15ml tablespoons. All cup and spoon measurements are level.

We use large eggs having an average weight of 60g.

how to measure

When using graduated metric measuring cups, shake dry ingredients loosely into the appropriate cup. Do not tap the cup on a bench or tightly pack the ingredients unless directed to do so. Level top of measuring cups and measuring spoons with a knife.
When measuring liquids, place a clear glass or plastic jug with metric markings on a flat surface to check accuracy at eye level.

index

Looking after **your interest...**

Keep your ACP cookbooks clean, tidy and within easy reach with a book holder designed to hold up to 12 books. Plus you can follow our recipes perfectly with a set of accurate measuring cups and spoons, as used by *The Australian Women's Weekly* Test Kitchen.

To order

Mail or fax Photocopy and complete the coupon below and post to ACP Books Reader Offer, ACP Publishing, GPO Box 4967, Sydney NSW 2001, or fax to (02) 9267 4967.

Phone Have your credit card details ready, then phone 136 116 (Mon-Fri, 8.00am-6.00pm; Sat, 8.00am-6.00pm).

Price

Book Holder

Australia: $13.10 (incl. GST).
Elsewhere: $A21.95.

Metric Measuring Set

Australia: $6.50 (incl. GST).
New Zealand: $A8.00.
Elsewhere: $A9.95.

Prices include postage and handling. This offer is available in all countries.

Payment

Australian residents

We accept the credit cards listed on the coupon, money orders and cheques.

Overseas residents

We accept the credit cards listed on the coupon, drafts in $A drawn on an Australian bank, and also UK, NZ and US cheques in the currency of the country of issue. Credit card charges are at the exchange rate current at the time of payment.

Test Kitchen
Food director *Pamela Clark*
Food editor *Karen Hammial*
Assistant food editor *Amira Georgy*
Test Kitchen managers *Kimberley Coverda,
Elizabeth Hooper*
Senior home economists *Kellie Ann*
Home economists *Kelly Cruikshanks,
Margaret Ientile, Cathie Lonnie,
Naomi Scesny, Jeanette Seamons,
Alison Webb, Danielle West*
Editorial coordinator *Rebecca Steyns*

ACP Books
Editorial director *Susan Tomnay*
Creative director *Hieu Chi Nguyen*
Senior editor *Julie Collard*
Designer *Mary Keep*
Pattern sheet *Ficope Graphic Services*
Sales director *Brian Cearnes*
Marketing director *Matt Dominello*
Brand manager *Renée Crea*
Production manager *Carol Currie*
Chief executive officer *John Alexander*
Group publisher *Pat Ingram*
Publisher *Sue Wannan*
Editorial director (AWW) *Deborah Thomas*

Produced by ACP Books, Sydney.
Printed by Dai Nippon Printing in Korea.
Published by ACP Publishing Pty Limited,
54 Park St, Sydney; GPO Box 4088,
Sydney, NSW 2001.
Ph: (02) 9282 8618 Fax: (02) 9267 9438.
acpbooks@acp.com.au
www.acpbooks.com.au
To order books, phone 136 116.
Send recipe enquiries to:
recipeenquiries@acp.com.au
RIGHTS ENQUIRIES
Laura Bamford, Director ACP Books.
lbamford@acplon.co.uk
Ph: +44 (207) 812 6526
AUSTRALIA: Distributed by Network Services,
GPO Box 4088, Sydney, NSW 2001.
Ph: (02) 9282 8777 Fax: (02) 9264 3278.
UNITED KINGDOM: Distributed by Australian
Consolidated Press (UK), Moulton Park
Business Centre, Red House Rd,
Moulton Park, Northampton, NN3 6AQ.
Ph: (01604) 497531 Fax: (01604) 497533
acpukltd@aol.com
CANADA: Distributed by Whitecap Books Ltd,
351 Lynn Ave, North Vancouver, BC, V7J 2C4.
Ph: (604) 980 9852 Fax: (604) 980 8197
customerservice@whitecap.ca
www.whitecap.ca
NEW ZEALAND: Distributed by Netlink
Distribution Company, ACP Media Centre,
Cnr Fanshawe and Beaumont Streets,
Westhaven, Auckland.
PO Box 47906, Ponsonby, Auckland, NZ.
Ph: (09) 366 9966 Fax: 0800 277 412
ask@ndcnz.co.nz
SOUTH AFRICA: Distributed by PSD Promotions,
30 Diesel Road Isando, Gauteng Johannesburg.
PO Box 1175, Isando 1600, Gauteng Johannesburg
Ph: (2711) 392 6065/6/7
Fax: (2711) 392 6079/80
orders@psdprom.co.za

Clark, Pamela.
Kids' birthday cakes.

Includes index.
ISBN 1 86396 281 6.

1. Birthday cakes. I. Title.
II Title: Australian Women's Weekly.

641.8653

Photocopy and complete coupon below

☐ **Book Holder**

☐ **Metric Measuring Set**
  Please indicate number(s) required.

Mr/Mrs/Ms _____

Address _____

_____

Postcode _____ Country _____

Ph: Business hours ( ) _____

I enclose my cheque/money order for $ _____
payable to ACP Publishing.

OR: please charge my

☐ Bankcard ☐ Visa ☐ Mastercard
☐ Diners Club ☐ American Express

| | | | | | | | | | | | | | | | | |
Card number

Expiry date ____ /____

Cardholder's signature _____

*Please allow up to 30 days delivery within Australia.
Allow up to 6 weeks for overseas deliveries.
Both offers expire 31/12/06. HLKBC05*